HSE BOOKS

THE PRINTER'S GUIDE TO HEALTH AND SAFETY

  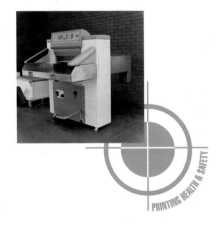

PRINTING HEALTH & SAFETY

First published 1998

ISBN 0 7176 1486 7

This guidance is prepared, in consultation with the Health and Safety Executive (HSE), by the Printing Industry Advisory Committee which was appointed by the Health and Safety Commission (HSC) as part of its formal advisory structures. The guidance represents what is considered to be good practice by the members of the Committee. It has been agreed by the Commission. Following the guidance is not compulsory and you are free to take other action. But if you do follow the guidance you will normally be doing enough to comply with the law. Health and safety inspectors seek to secure compliance with the law and may refer to this guidance as illustrating good practice.

WHAT IS PIAC?

The Printing Industry Advisory Committee (PIAC) was formed in July 1979 to advise the Health and Safety Commission (HSC) on matters concerning the printing industry. The members of PIAC are nominated by the CBI and the TUC and appointed by HSC to work together with HSE to advise the industry on health and safety.

Why does PIAC exist?

Every year people are seriously injured working in the printing industry. Many others suffer ill health which prevents them from doing their normal work. Almost all of these cases could be prevented.

PIAC is determined to take action to improve health and safety performance in the printing industry. As part of this process PIAC has developed this guidance book to help those responsible for health and safety in the industry understand their responsibilities and take the necessary action.

This is the core book in a new series of health and safety guidance for printing. The series will be developed over the next few years. The aim of the series is to help all those involved in printing, including employers, employees and suppliers, to identify the main causes of accidents and ill health and to explain how to eliminate the hazards and control the risks. Every book in the series will be identified by the logo on the front cover.

ACKNOWLEDGEMENTS

Assistance from the following in providing photographs is gratefully acknowledged:

Matthews the Printers

Harnsworth Quays Printing Limited

Delta Displays

Heidelberg Graphic Equipment

Printo Wrappings

MEMBERS OF THE PRINTING INDUSTRY ADVISORY COMMITTEE

MEMBERS OF PIAC PRINTER'S GUIDE WORKING PARTY

CONTENTS

■ ■ ■ ■ ■ ■ ■ ■ ■ ■ ■

CHAPTER 4 HEALTH RISKS

INTRODUCTION

Every year people are seriously injured and made ill working in printing. This book has been written for people who manage and work in the industry. It is designed to help them effectively manage health, safety and welfare in printing to comply with their responsibilities and to reduce accidents and ill health.

There are legal requirements that you have to meet and these are outlined in this book, along with important practical advice on health and safety issues in the printing industry.

As printing is a wide-ranging activity, this book does not deal with every hazard which may arise or every precaution that can be taken. It does, however, outline some of the more serious and frequent hazards and ways of dealing with them.

Looking at your business in the way this book suggests will help you stay safe. It will go a long way to satisfying the law - including the risk assessments that you must do under the Management of Health and Safety at Work Regulations 1992.

There are 'Relevant legislation' sections at the start of each chapter which list the acts, regulations etc which apply and may also contain summaries of the main legal requirements. These sections have a blue background.

You may find this book tells you all you need to know, but if not, the References section will help you find out more. This is structured in chapter order to make it easier to use. See the 'How to obtain publications' section for useful addresses.

The law and guidance

The term 'reasonably practicable' is used in much of UK health and safety law and will be found in this book. This means that the degree of risk in a particular job or workplace needs to be balanced against the time, trouble, cost and physical difficulty of taking measures to avoid or reduce the risk. In other words, it would have to be shown that a particular risk is insignificant in relation to the sacrifice needed to reduce it. This book will help you in deciding what is reasonably practicable for your company.

The word 'must' indicates a definite legal requirement. 'Do's and 'don'ts', 'shoulds' and 'should nots' and other recommendations represent best and good practice which will lead to compliance with what is reasonably practicable. However, there may be other legally acceptable ways of achieving the same objective. Requirements of an approved code of practice (ACOP) have a special status in law; a court will find fault if you have not followed the code or done something equally effective.

'Think about', 'consider' and similar phrases contain a tip or hint which may not amount to a precise legal requirement but indicate an approach to a health and safety problem which ought to be considered.

A 'safeguard' is a means of reducing risk to health and/or safety.

Chapter 1

MANAGING HEALTH AND SAFETY

■ ■ ■ ■ ■ ■ ■ ■ ■ ■ ■

See the References section at the back of the book for details of publications which relate to MANAGING HEALTH AND SAFETY

Relevant legislation

The Health and Safety at Work etc Act 1974 and the Management of Health and Safety at Work Regulations 1992 place duties on companies and individuals to ensure that adequate provisions are made for health and safety at work. Directors, managers and other responsible people all have duties under the Act. Commitment to the effective management of health and safety should come from the top.

You must ensure, so far as is reasonably practicable, the health, safety and welfare of your employees and any others who may be affected by what you do. This will include those who work for you as casual workers, part-timers, trainees and others who visit your premises, for example customers or contractors. It will also include those who may be affected by what you do, eg neighbours, clients, sales people, members of the public and those who use products or equipment you make, supply or import.

In addition, employers must:

● identify the measures they need to take by carrying out a risk assessment (and if you employ five or more you will need to record the main findings);

● have a written health and safety policy (if you employ five or more people);

● have adequate arrangements for health and safety and, in particular, for the effective planning, organisation, control, monitoring and review of the preventive measures required under health and safety law;

● provide employees with any necessary information and training in safe practices;

● appoint one or more competent persons to assist them in taking the measures necessary to comply with their legal duties (a competent person is regarded as a person who has had sufficient training, experience or knowledge and other qualities to enable them to properly assist in undertaking these measures).

Setting the policy

If you employ five or more people, you must have a written statement of your health and safety policy. It needs to be a carefully prepared, well thought-out and up-to-date document based on commitment at senior management level.

The policy should be specific to your firm, setting out your general policy for protecting the health and safety of your employees at work and specifying the organisation and arrangements for putting the policy into practice. The primary purpose of this document is to set out your basic action plan on health and safety and it should lead to better standards in the workplace.

The policy needs to:

- state what your general aims are with regard to your employees' health and safety. The statement should be signed and dated by senior management to make the firm's commitment to the policy clear;

- clearly show where the duties for health and safety lie. While the overall responsibility for health and safety rests at the highest management level, individuals at every level will have to accept some responsibility for carrying out the policy;

- describe the systems and procedures in place for ensuring the health and safety of your employees. This could be linked with your risk assessment in which you will have considered the risk that arise in your workplace and taken action to control them. Your arrangements for seeing that the rules and instructions set out in the policy are followed by your employees should also be laid down;

- be brought to the notice of your employees, for example by giving them a copy;

- be revised if the organisation changes or new hazards arise;

- be supported by sufficient resources, eg enough finance, people and time to translate the policy into action.

Organising the staff

The four 'Cs' of a positive health and safety culture are:

- competence - in recruitment, training and advisory support;

- control - by allocating responsibilities and securing commitment;

- co-operation - between individuals and groups;

- communication - including oral, written and visible forms.

Ask yourself:

- Have you allocated responsibilities for health and safety to specific people?

- Do you consult and involve your staff and the safety representatives effectively? (See the 'Consulting employees on health and safety' section later in this chapter.)

- Do your staff have sufficient information about the risks they run and the preventive measures?

- Do you have the right levels of expertise? Are your people properly trained? (See the following chapter.)

- Do you need specialist advice from outside the organisation and have you arranged to obtain it?

Planning and risk assessment

Systematic planning for health and safety is needed so that hazards can be identified, risks assessed, control measures and priorities determined and the necessary resources allocated. Ask yourself:

- Do you have a health and safety plan?

- Is health and safety always considered before any new work is started?

- Have you identified hazards and assessed risks to your own staff and the public, and set standards for premises, plant, substances, procedures, people and products?

- Do you have a plan to deal with serious or imminent dangers, eg fires, process deviations etc?

- Are the standards implemented and risks effectively controlled?

The Management of Health and Safety at Work Regulations 1992 set out broad general duties aimed at improving health and safety management. Among other things, they require precautions to be identified by means of risk assessments carried out in the workplace and a competent person to be appointed to assist the employers in carrying out their duties under health and safety law.

Risk assessment

The purpose of risk assessment is to help the employer or self-employed person to determine what measures should be taken to comply with legal duties. This includes general duties under the Health and Safety at Work etc Act 1974 and the more specific

duties in the various acts and regulations. Once determined, action will need to be taken to implement the necessary preventive and protective measures.

The risk assessment needs to consider:

- the level of risk;

- who might be harmed;

- whether the significant risks are being adequately controlled.

A hazard is anything with the potential to cause harm and risk is the chance of harm actually being done. For example, a can of highly flammable liquid stored in a closed metal cabinet in a workroom is a flammable hazard due to the nature of the liquid but little risk due to the storage arrangements. The risk increases if the liquid is poured into an open container before use because there is then a danger of spillage. The risk significantly increases if people are smoking in the area.

The following five steps need to be followed when carrying out a risk assessment:

Step 1 Identify the hazards

- Take a careful look at the workplace and the work activities, including make-ready, cleaning, maintenance, repair, hickey picking and normal running. Do any of these present a health or safety hazard?

- Think about what can reasonably be foreseen as likely to cause harm, such as contra-rotating rollers, including inking rollers and print cylinders, or hazardous chemicals. (See Chapter 5 for more information on machinery hazards.)

- Consider what the worst result could be, eg a badly trapped finger or a fatality.

Step 2 Decide who might be harmed and how

- Consider how many people could be hurt if things go wrong, including employees, particularly unfamiliar or untrained operators, visitors and members of the public.

- Do not overlook maintenance staff and contractors.

Step 3 Evaluate the risks arising from the hazards and take the necessary remedial action

- Ask whether existing precautions are enough to protect people and, if they are not, what more needs to be done. Take account of workers who may be distracted. Check existing safeguards are well designed. Badly designed guards and those that are inconvenient to use or can be easily defeated may not be maintained. If in doubt, upgrade to a better standard and in the short term ensure regular checks are carried out to verify guards etc are being used correctly.

- Use recognised industry standards, such as publications from the Health and Safety Executive (HSE), PIAC and the British Printing Industries Federation (BPIF) as a yardstick.

- Refer to suppliers' instructions and data sheets.

- Ask yourself whether the precautions you have in place comply with the law, represent good practice and reduce risk so far as is reasonably practicable.

- Prioritise your actions.

- Allocate necessary resources.

- Implement procedures to ensure necessary work will be completed.

Step 4: Record your findings

If you have five or more employees you must record the significant findings of your assessment. (An example risk assessment form is given in Appendix 2, a schematic diagram of example points to consider in an assessment of a small printing premises is given in Appendix 3.)

Step 5: Review your assessment

You will also need to revise it when necessary. Once improvements have been made, remember that things change and you need to check regularly that precautions remain in place.

Monitoring

Your safety policy can include arrangements for monitoring. Monitoring is also a requirement under the Management of Health and Safety at Work Regulations 1992. As part of monitoring the safety policy and arrangements, spot checks or fuller inspections can be made. Reports of all accidents, near misses and ill health caused by work should be studied and a watch should be kept for trends or patterns.

Systems need to be in place to control and monitor risks and proper safeguards need to be adopted and maintained. Monitoring is a management responsibility and, in order to manage health and safety successfully, firms will need an effective monitoring and follow-up system.

Inspection and checks

Monitoring can be carried out by several different methods, for example:

- routine checks by managers, supervisors and maintenance staff, eg tours of inspection;

- statutory tests and examinations by competent persons, eg of lift truck chains, lifting equipment, and pressure systems by engineering surveyors;

- reporting of defects by employees, eg operator daily/weekly inspection of machinery safeguards;

- health surveillance by a competent person, eg inspecting hands of printers who work with UV cured inks for signs of dermatitis;

- investigation of incidents and monitoring of reports to identify reasons for failures in controls and the steps needed to prevent a recurrence.

Evaluation of accidents, ill health and near misses

An effective system for recording all relevant incidents is important. Records of accidents/ill health and near misses can be used to identify problem areas and take relevant action. A lack of accidents does not necessarily mean all is well, good luck may have been playing a role.

Detailed investigation of incidents helps to identify underlying causes. It will help to highlight weaknesses or omissions in the firm's current safety standards or policy. The findings can be used to help prevent recurrence and initiate the necessary remedial action (which should be carried out promptly).

Auditing and review

Health and safety auditing aims to provide a comprehensive, independent check of work activities and of the existing arrangements for managing and monitoring health and safety in order to identify shortcomings. It provides feedback to managers on how well risks are being controlled. Auditing is usually most effective when it is carried out by people independent of the areas being audited, eg from another department or site.

Auditing schemes can be developed in-house or commercially available schemes can be used. A number of consultants also operate schemes but printing firms need to satisfy themselves that a consultant is appropriate, sufficiently qualified and competent to help in their particular operation.

The information obtained from measuring safety performance and auditing can be used to review how well you are doing and what might need improvement.

Accidents and emergencies

As an employer in the printing industry you need to put into place suitable arrangements for identifying, recording and investigating all relevant accidents and incidents. Certain accidents, dangerous occurrences and incidences of ill health are also reportable.

The law and reporting accidents

The Reporting of Injuries, Diseases and Dangerous Occurrences Regulations 1995 (RIDDOR) require you to report certain accidents, incidents and occupational diseases to your enforcing authority within specified time limits. This will usually be HSE but may be your local authority. RIDDOR applies to all employers and the self-employed and covers everyone at work (including those on work experience and similar schemes).

RIDDOR requires you to:

- Keep details of the incident (eg in your accident book).

- Notify your enforcing authority immediately (eg by telephone) if any of the following happen as a result of work:

  - anybody dies;

  - an employee receives a major injury (such as a broken arm or leg or an amputation injury) or any other person is taken to hospital immediately as a result of an injury caused by your work activities;

  - anyone is seriously affected by an electric shock or poisoning;

  - if there is a dangerous occurrence, eg a fire or explosion which stops work for more than 24 hours, or a crane overturns.

  Confirm the report in writing within ten days using the prescribed form F2508.

- Report within ten days (on form F2508) accidents at work which result in an employee being absent from work (or unable to do their normal job) for more than three days.

- Report certain diseases suffered by workers who do specified types of work as soon as possible on receiving a written diagnosis about the illness from a medical practitioner. The prescribed form F2508A should be used.

A leaflet *Everyone's guide to RIDDOR* (HSE31) contains more information and fuller definitions of classes of reportable incidents. If you need to report a serious incident outside office hours you can still obtain an emergency contact number by telephoning your local HSE office.

Investigating accidents and emergencies

Investigation of accidents and incidents in-house is important to establish causes and preventive measures needed to minimise the risk of further accidents. You should also look at near misses, minor accidents and property damage. It is often only by good fortune that someone is not injured. Employers need to put procedures in place to ensure the following stages are followed in the event of an accident or dangerous occurrence:

- Take any action required to deal with the immediate risks, eg provide first aid, put out the fire, isolate any danger, fence off the area, call the emergency services.

- If the incident is one that must be immediately notified to your enforcing authority, consult them before disturbing the site. Even if the incident is not reportable, it is sensible to take photographs and measurements before disturbing the site.

- Obtain basic facts, eg witness names, plant condition, substances in use, place, time, extent of injury.

- Establish the circumstances, eg what was being done at the time and what happened, the experience of the people involved etc. Most accidents have more than one cause so don't be too quick to blame individuals - try to look at and deal with any root causes, eg lack of training.

- Identify preventive measures, eg assess/reassess the risk, reappraise intended safeguards and work methods, check PIAC guidance.

- Establish whether the initial management response was adequate, eg whether there was effective first-aid response or correct spillage procedures were used.

- Identify the underlying causes, such as management or supervision failures,

inadequate training or poor maintenance.

- Take steps to stop something similar from happening again. In deciding the right course of action think about whether the outcome could have been more serious and what prevented this from happening.

- Remember you have a duty to carry out risk assessments for your work under the Management of Health and Safety at Work Regulations 1992. Although accidents can indicate where risk assessment needs to be reviewed, you should not wait for the accident to happen before you do the risk assessment.

The investigation checklist shown opposite may be useful. Although it is not an exhaustive list, it gives examples of questions that might be relevant.

Dealing with emergencies

When things go wrong people may be exposed to serious and immediate danger. Special procedures are necessary to deal with emergencies such as serious injuries, explosion, fire, flood, poisoning, electrocution, power failures, chemical spills or even a radioactive leak.

You should prepare an emergency plan if a major incident at your workplace could involve risks to the public, rescuing employees or co-ordination of the emergency services.

To do this you should carry out a risk assessment and consider:

- the worst that could happen;

- how people - those in charge and others - will deal with the problems. (Have you identified and addressed training needs and allocated responsibilities?);

- how the emergency services should get access onto the site;

- how the alarm will be raised (don't forget night and shift working, weekends and holidays);

- how and when to call the emergency services and how to assist them with information when they arrive;

Investigation checklist

DO YOU NEED TO:	YES	NO
Improve physical safeguards, eg provide an interlocked guard?		
Provide and use local exhaust ventilation?		
Use mechanical handling aids, eg pile turners or mobile lifts?		
Introduce better test and maintenance arrangements?		
Improve work methods?		
Provide and use personal protective equipment?		
Make changes to supervision and training arrangements?		
Review similar risks in other departments?		
Set up systems to risk assess new plant and chemicals before use?		
Review procedures for contractors?		
Update standards and policies?		
Introduce monitoring and auditing systems?		
Give training in manual handling techniques?		
Substitute chemicals with something less hazardous?		
Change make-ready procedures or other systems of work?		
Institute health surveillance, eg for UV ink users?		

- that you will need to notify the fire authority if you have over 25 tonnes of certain dangerous substances on site;

- where to go to reach a place of safety or to get rescue equipment;

- providing emergency lighting;

- whether you have sufficient emergency exits to allow everyone to escape quickly (and suitable arrangements to ensure that emergency doors and escape routes are kept unobstructed and clearly marked at all times);

- nominating competent persons to take control;

- pre-planning and practising emergency plant shutdowns or making processes safe. Important items such as shut-off valves, electrical isolators etc should be clearly labelled to avoid confusion;

- ensuring you have adequate first-aid provisions and first aiders;

- training people in emergency and evacuation procedures and remembering the needs of people with disabilities.

First aid

The Health and Safety (First-Aid) Regulations 1981 require you to have adequate arrangements for first aid.

The minimum first-aid provision for each work site is:

- a person appointed to take charge of first-aid arrangements including looking after the equipment and facilities and calling the emergency services when required. An appointed person will need to be available whenever people are at work;

- a suitably stocked first-aid container (easily accessible in cases of emergency);

- information for employees on first-aid arrangements (including notices telling people where the first-aid equipment, facilities and personnel can be found).

Additional provision will be appropriate in many cases, for example:

- If the risks of injury and ill health arising from the work as identified in your risk assessment are significant, trained first aiders may be needed. They may also be needed where large numbers of people are employed.

They must be given the right training and hold a certificate (which will be valid for three years). Refresher courses and re-examination will be required when old certificates expire. Information on training courses and organisations can be obtained from your local Employment Medical Advisory Service (who can be contacted via your local HSE office).

- Where there are specific risks from working with hazardous substances, dangerous machinery and loads, consider specific training for first aiders, extra first-aid equipment, siting of first-aid equipment, informing emergency services and first-aid rooms.

- Where workplaces are remote from emergency medical services, inform local medical services of your location and consider special arrangements with them.

- Where you have inexperienced workers, disabled workers or personnel with special health problems, consider the needs for special equipment and local siting of equipment.

If fully trained first aiders are not appropriate in view of the small size and the nature of the risks of your company, emergency first aiders could be appropriate (training for emergency first aiders involves a one-day course).

As your company grows you will need to look at your first-aid needs again. Further guidance on your first-aid responsibilities can be found in the Approved Code of Practice entitled *First aid at work. Health and Safety (First-Aid) Regulations 1981 Approved Code of Practice and guidance on regulations* (L74).

Contracted work can be small or large scale

Control of contractors

Contractors are routinely employed to work in the printing industry, particularly on the maintenance, modification or installation of plant and equipment, eg for machinery maintenance, maintenance of the electrical installation, decoration of premises and work on fragile roofs. Everyone working on your premises needs to know what health and safety standards they have to achieve, including labour-only contractors.

The law and managing contractors

The Health and Safety at Work etc Act 1974 places duties on you and your contractor to protect, so far as is reasonably practicable, the health and safety of employees and other people who may be affected by your work activities. All parties will need to co-operate with each other and co-ordinate their work to

ensure everyone is complying with their legal duties.

In addition to the Health and Safety at Work etc Act 1974 and the Management of Health and Safety at Work Regulations 1992, you should be aware of the Construction (Design and Management) Regulations 1994. These Regulations place duties on clients, clients' agents, designers and contractors to plan their approach and take health and safety into account. Health and safety needs to be co-ordinated and managed effectively throughout all stages of a construction project, from conception through to subsequent maintenance and repair arrangements.

Clients must be reasonably satisfied that they only use competent people as planning supervisors, designers and principal contractors. They also need to be satisfied that sufficient resources, including time, have been or will be allocated to enable the project to be carried out in compliance with health and safety law.

The Regulations apply where construction work is expected to last more than 30 days and involve five or more people on-site. This will include the installation of fixed plant where persons are liable to fall more than 2 m, such as installation of larger web-fed presses. The Regulations apply regardless of the length of time or the number of people carrying out the work where demolition or dismantling of a structure is taking place.

For further information see *A guide to the Construction Health, Safety and Welfare) Regulations 1996* (INDG220) and the Approved Code of Practice on the Construction (Design and Management) Regulations 1994 (L54).

Before selecting the contractor

Contractors should be made fully aware of the standards of health and safety management you expect of them. In order to select suitable contractors, you will need to:

- assess their competence in health and safety matters. This applies to senior people as well as those working on-site;

- where appropriate, assess their organisation and arrangements. Does their safety policy adequately cover hazards that will be met while carrying out work at your site? Do they carry out effective risk assessment?

- assess their performance.

Planning the work

Pre-contract meetings may be needed to discuss working arrangements, eg safe systems of work and method statements, and to carry out risk assessments. Consider:

- implementation of safe systems of work, such as hot work or work on fragile roofs;

- your own operations which may affect the contractor's work;

- what tools, plant, substances and equipment will be used;

- what the arrangements for proper supervision will be. Who will be keeping an eye on contractors on-site to ensure they are accounted for, eg in the event of fire, and to make sure they are following the procedures that have been laid down?

- the health and safety issues when setting down working methods. Detailed written procedures (method statements or permit-to-work systems) will be appropriate for complicated or hazardous operations.

Make sure that the contractor's employees understand your rules for safe working, as well as the hazards and precautions, and that you understand theirs. Each new employee coming onto site should receive appropriate instruction and training and be familiarised with your workplace and emergency plans, eg fire and medical emergency procedures.

Control of contractors on-site

Appoint a competent, suitably trained person (this could be a manager, a company safety officer or chief engineer) to liaise with the contractor and monitor their actual health and safety performance. Ensure that you and the contractor keep each other informed about hazards and changes to plans or systems of work which may affect health and safety.

Consulting employees on health and safety

By law, employers must consult all of their employees on health and safety matters. Where employers have recognised unions the Safety Representatives and Safety Committees Regulations 1977 will apply. Where employees are not members of a union, or the union are not recognised, the Health and Safety (Consultation with Employees) Regulations 1996 (HSCER) will apply.

Consultation with employees must be carried out on matters to do with their health and safety at work, including:

- any change that may substantially affect their health and safety at work, eg in procedures, equipment or ways of working such as safe systems of work for cleaning printing cylinders;

- the employer's arrangements for getting competent people to help him or her satisfy health and safety laws;

- the information that employees must be given on the likely risks and dangers arising from their work, for example fire and explosion hazards when using highly flammable inks, measures to reduce or get rid of these risks, and what they should do if they have to deal with a risk or danger;

- the planning of health and safety training; and

- the health and safety consequences of introducing new technology, for example use of UV inks.

Further information on consulting employees is available in the free leaflet *Consulting employees on health and safety: a guide to the law* (INDG232).

Under the Safety Representatives and Safety Committees Regulations 1977, trade union appointed safety representatives have the right to:

- investigate potential hazards and dangerous occurrences;

- examine the causes of accidents;

- investigate complaints by employees relating to health and safety;

- make representation to their employer on health and safety matters;

- carry out inspection of the workplace;

- receive time off with pay to perform these functions and undergo training.

Employers have a general duty to consult safety representatives on all aspects of health and safety in the workplace, and provide them with the necessary information, facilities and assistance to permit them to carry out their functions. This is with a view to making and maintaining arrangements for their joint co-operation in the promotion and development of measures to ensure employees' health and safety at work, and to check the effectiveness of such measures.

A safety committee must be established if requested in writing by two safety representatives. The employer should then consult with the safety representatives and establish the safety committee no later than three months after the request was made. A notice should be posted for employees stating the composition of the committee.

Further information can be found in the priced publication *Safety representatives and safety committees* (L87), known as the 'Brown Book'.

Inspectors and enforcement

Enforcement for health and safety at work lies with either inspectors from HSE or from your local authority. Health and safety in printing and many allied trades is normally enforced by HSE inspectors.

An inspector's primary function is to ensure that there are acceptable standards of health and safety in the workplace.

In order to aid enforcing authorities in carrying out their duties, you are required by law to notify your enforcing authority (normally your local HSE office) that you are occupying a factory or office.

Powers of inspectors

Inspectors have powers of enforcement which include:

- issuing improvement notices requiring improvements to be made within a certain time;

- issuing prohibition notices stopping a process or the use of a piece of equipment where a risk of serious personal injury exists;

- prosecution of a business, or under certain circumstances an individual, for breaches of health and safety law.

They may visit to inspect the workplace or to investigate accidents or complaints. They often visit workplaces without giving notice but you are entitled to see their identification before letting them in. Their powers include right of entry into your premises, the right to talk to employees and safety representatives and to take photographs and samples. They are entitled to your co-operation and answers to questions.

Inspectors will enforce the law when they judge it necessary but they are concerned to help you do what is reasonable and practicable to control risks to health and safety. They will give advice and you may turn to them for guidance. They are happy to answer questions and give you information and a lot of the information sheets, leaflets etc are free. You can also contact your local HSE office or, for general enquiries, HSE's InfoLine - telephone 0541 545500.

Chapter 2

TRINING

▪ ▪ ▪ ▪ ▪ ▪ ▪ ▪ ▪ ▪ ▪ ▪

See the References section at the back of the book for details of publications which relate to TRAINING

Relevant legislation

Training requirements are identified in several acts and regulations including the following:

- The Health and Safety at Work etc Act 1974

- The Management of Health and Safety at Work Regulations 1992

- The Provision and Use of Work Equipment Regulations 1992

- The Control of Substances Hazardous to Health Regulations 1994

- The Electricity at Work Regulations 1989

Ensure that all employees, including supervisors and managers, have adequate health and safety training.

Training methods

These will vary for different people and jobs depending on existing abilities and the risks of the job. Any training provider needs to be a competent trainer.

Training can be carried out by one or more of the following:

- in-house training personnel (these might include supervisors);

- external trainers (this can be done on the premises or by sending employees away on short courses or day release courses);

- distance and open learning techniques;

- training provided by suppliers and manufacturers following installation of new or refurbished machinery;

- 'sitting with Nellie' - the experienced operator should be assessed as competent both in the job and as a teacher of its health and safety aspects to avoid teaching bad habits.

Training materials are available from a number of sources including the Printing Industry Advisory Committee (PIAC), trade organisations, safety organisations such as the British Safety Council and the Royal Society for the Prevention of Accidents, and independent training and health and safety consultants.

Training and enterprise councils (TECs) in England and Wales and local enterprise companies (LECs) in Scotland are able to provide practical help on training. They can also provide information on National and Scottish Vocational Qualifications (NVQs and SVQs) which meet standards of competence laid down for particular jobs.

Induction training

Induction training for new employees will help them settle into their new work situation. This type of training usually includes information about the company, the organisation for managing health and safety, the hazards of the workplace, the principles of safe working practice and the safety responsibilities of individuals under the law.

Managers and supervisors have a key responsibility for maintaining a safe working environment. They are accountable for the safety of those under their control. Supervisors have the task of spotting hazards and investigating accidents and near misses. They should be trained to identify unsafe systems of work and to put them right.

Senior managers need to know enough about health and safety matters to determine priorities and to assess the performance of people further down the management line. They should examine the health and safety training needs of individuals at regular intervals. Their commitment to training should be identified in the company safety policy.

After induction the individual health and safety needs of the employees should be appraised and met to enable each person to work safely. No-one should be asked to perform tasks for which they have not been trained.

The following are examples of the topics appropriate for inclusion in induction training at different levels within a company:

Training for all employees - example topics

- Company structure

- Company safety policy

- Safety committees

- Safety representatives

- Occupational health arrangements

- Responsibilities of individuals

- Company rules

- Hazards and safe working standards
  - Housekeeping
  - Machinery
  - Visual display units (VDUs)
  - Fire
  - Chemicals
  - Materials handling
  - Electricity
  - Noise
  - First aid

Training for all supervisors/managers - example topics

- Responsibilities

- Monitoring of health and safety standards

- Hazard identification

- Accident investigations/reports

- Risk assessment

- Relevant legal requirements

- Precautions

- Sources of information

Training for senior managers - example topics

- Purpose of company health and safety policy

- Causes of accidents/ill health and their costs

- Planning for health and safety

- Monitoring accidents, reports and statistics

- Personal accountability

- Functions of safety committees and safety representatives

- Developing a safety culture

- Use of safety audits

- Relevant legal requirements

- Role of safety adviser

- Knowledge of the work of HSE

- Role of the Occupational Health Service

- Existence of relevant standards and guidance

Other types of training

Job specific

There are many hazardous activities in the printing industry where specific job training in safe systems of work etc is essential, eg press cleaning, webbing-up, guillotine operating, maintenance work, lift trucks, manual handling.

Training for employees moving jobs

Inform all employees of the dangers associated with a new job and give them training in the precautions to be taken. Even experienced employees may need training when they are moved to new areas of work or asked to operate new types of machines.

Refresher training

Retraining should be carried out on a regular basis, to reinforce particular safety issues, and when there are changes in the process, equipment or law. Sometimes accident investigations can reveal the need for retraining.

Training of safety representatives

Trade union appointed safety representatives have two distinct training needs. Firstly, they need to understand their functions as a trade union official and to do this they are entitled to time off with pay to attend a TUC or other approved trade union course.

Secondly, they may need additional training in the particular hazards of the industry - not only the hazards inherent in their own jobs but also the hazards of work undertaken by the people they represent. The employer has duties towards safety representatives (see the 'Consulting employees on health and safety' section in Chapter 1). Companies should assist in ensuring that trade union appointed safety representatives in their company receive adequate training on industry hazards and the rules and the procedures operating within their own company to control such hazards.

Reviewing training needs

Training needs should be regularly reviewed to check that the training delivered is adequate. Training needs can also be reviewed when investigating accidents, investigating near misses and as a result of carrying out risk assessment.

ACCIDENTS

Job specific

The operator of an offset litho printing machine was killed when his pullover was caught by the inking rollers causing strangulation. He was trying to retrieve misfed paper via the gap beneath the duct keys below the inking rollers guard. The guard was deficient and the operator did not turn the machine off before attempting retrieval. Training should have been given in the safe method of working and the required standard of machinery guarding. Procedures should have been in place to check the condition of guards regularly.

A machine operator in a printing works damaged his spine when he fell from a ladder while carrying out maintenance work at high level machinery. The ladder was not tied or footed. Operators regularly carried out minor maintenance work but none had been trained in the use of ladders.

Training for those moving jobs

An experienced printer had part of his right index finger amputated while changing the blade of a guillotine he had not operated before and had not been trained to use.

Refresher training

A printing shop supervisor trapped two fingers in a folding machine while clearing a creased piece of paper without stopping the machine. He had been fully trained some years previously but had short-circuited the safe work procedures so frequently without incident that he no longer recognised the obvious risk.

Training

Chapter 3

WORKPLACE AND TRANSPORT SAFETY

■ ■ ■ ■ ■ ■ ■ ■ ■ ■ ■ ■ ■

See the References section at the back of the book for details of publications which relate to WORKPLACE AND TRANSPORT SAFETY

Relevant legislation

General requirements for workplace and transport safety are contained in a number of acts and regulations such as the Health and Safety at Work etc Act 1974 and the Management of Health and Safety Regulations 1992.

The Workplace (Health Safety and Welfare) Regulations 1992 are specifically aimed at protecting the health and safety of everyone in the workplace, and ensuring that adequate welfare facilities are provided for people at work. Employers have duties to ensure that workplaces under their control comply with these Regulations. More detailed information can be found below and in the publication *Workplace health, safety and welfare. Workplace (Health, Safety and Welfare) Regulations 1992. Approved Code of Practice and guidance* (L24).

The Disability Discrimination Act 1995 creates a right of non-discrimination against disabled people in the field of employment, including a duty on employers to provide 'reasonable adjustment' to working conditions or the working environment to overcome the practical effects of disability. Employers are not expected to make any changes which would break health and safety laws.

The employment part of the Disability Discrimination Act does not apply to employers who employ fewer than 20 people. However, they are encouraged to follow good practice guidelines. Further information on the Disability Discrimination Act should be obtained from the Department of Education and Employment (see the phone book for the number of your local office).

Fundamentals of workplace health and safety

Some of the basic requirements for employers are outlined below:

Safe place of work

You must have:

- buildings in good repair;

- precautions where people or materials might fall from open edges, eg mezzanine floors, racking areas and running boards;

- space for safe movement and access, eg around reelstands and on mezzanine floors;

- floors, corridors and stairs etc free from obstructions, eg trailing cables and pallets;

- good drainage in wet processes, eg

screen cleaning in screen printing or flexographic printing using water-based inks;

- windows that can be opened and cleaned safely including roof lights. You may need to fit anchor points if window cleaners need to use harnesses;

- weather protection for those working outdoors, eg lift truck drivers, security guards, traffic controllers (banksmen) and delivery workers;

- outdoor routes kept safe during icy conditions, eg salted, sanded and swept.

Also think about:

- machinery and furniture being sited so that sharp corners do not stick out, eg at buckle-folders;

- not overloading floors - presses, particularly old ones, are very heavy;

- space for storing tools and materials.

Lighting

You must provide:

- good light. Use natural light where possible but try to avoid glare;

- a good level of local lighting at workstations;

- suitable forms of lighting. Some fluorescent tubes flicker and can be dangerous, giving some rotating machinery the appearance of being stationary;

- well lit outside areas - this will help security.

You will need special fittings for flammable or explosive atmospheres, eg at heat-set ovens, flexo and gravure presses (see the 'Explosion risks in flexo and gravure' section in Chapter 7).

Think about light-coloured walls to make the most of natural and artificial light.

Moving around the premises

You must have:

- safe passage for pedestrians and vehicles. You may need clearly marked separate routes (see the section on 'Safe movement of vehicles' later in this chapter);

- level, even surfaces without holes or broken boards;

- hand-rails on stairs and ramps where necessary;

- safe doors, eg vision panels in swing doors and sensitive edges on power doors;

- surfaces which are not slippery.

Think about marking steps, kerbs and fixed obstacles, eg by black and yellow diagonal stripes.

Designing workstations

When designing workstations and seating arrangements, consider comfort and safety. Ergonomic principles should be followed and adequate account taken of responsibilities under the Manual Handling Regulations 1992 and the Health and Safety (Display Screen Equipment) Regulations 1992. This advice applies to the hand-working and insertion sectors in particular.

Workstations and seating must fit the worker and the work. Seating must be provided where the work operations (or substantial parts of the operations) can or must be done sitting. Seating should also be provided for employees whose work necessitates them having to stand for long periods.

Cleanliness

You must:

- provide clean floors and stairs which are not slippery;

- provide clean premises, furniture and fittings (eg lights);

- provide containers for waste materials, eg metal-lidded bins for wash-up rags;

- remove dirt, refuse and trade waste regularly - remember to notify laundries if they are receiving solvent or UV ink-laden rags;

- clear up spillage promptly and arrange proper disposal, eg through a licensed contractor;

- keep internal walls or ceilings clean. They may need painting to help easy cleaning.

Hygiene and welfare

You must provide:

- clean, well ventilated toilets (separate for men and women unless each toilet has its own lockable door);

- wash basins with hot and cold (or warm) running water;

- soap and towels (or a hand dryer);

- skin cleansers, with nail brushes where necessary;

- barrier cream and skin conditioning cream where necessary;

- drying facilities for wet clothes;

- certain facilities for workers working away from base;

- lockers or hanging space for clothing;

- changing facilities where special clothing is worn;

- a clean drinking water supply (marked if necessary to distinguish it from the non-drinkable supply);

- rest facilities, such as rest rooms or rest areas, including suitable facilities to eat meals where food eaten in the workplace would otherwise become contaminated - the ACOP (L24) outlines additional arrangements, eg for heating food;

- arrangements to protect non-smokers from discomfort caused by tobacco smoke in any separate rest areas, eg provide separate areas or rooms for smokers and non-smokers or prohibit

smoking in rest areas and rest rooms;

- rest facilities for pregnant women and nursing mothers;

- adequate temperature and ventilation including fresh air. The ACOP (L24) refers to a minimum temperature of 16°C unless the work involves a lot of severe physical effort, in which case the temperature should be at least 13°C.

Safe movement of vehicles

Many accidents each year involve powered vehicles including lorries, vans and lift trucks. Injuries may be severe, and even fatal. Transport movements in and around the workplace need to be controlled to protect pedestrians, and to prevent damage to plant and equipment such as racking systems. Risk assessments need to take account of any contractors who may work on, or visit the site. Contract loaders in the newspaper industry are one example of this.

Look at the movement of goods around, into and off the site. For example, check that:

- vehicles and pedestrians are separated as much as possible. Traffic routes used by both need to be wide enough to enable vehicles to pass pedestrians safely. Barriers or rails may be needed in particularly vulnerable places, such as doorways, gateways, tunnels, bridges or other enclosed routes;

- pedestrian access to loading bays and delivery points is controlled;

- areas in which vehicles are moved are well lit;

- workstations, vulnerable plant, gas containers and chemical storage facilities are not likely to be struck during vehicle movements;

- traffic routes, roadways and pedestrian routes are clearly marked;

- site speed limits are marked and observed;

- speed control measures, such as humps, are provided where appropriate (gaps may be needed to allow lift trucks to pass safely);

- safe crossing points for pedestrians are marked;

- action is taken to control danger at blind spots, including openings with strip curtains which vehicles travel through or past;

- visiting drivers know and follow your rules;

- if necessary, vehicle movements are directly supervised by properly trained signallers (banksmen), particularly when reversing and near blind corners;

- banksmen are visible to drivers at all times, and are able to stand in a safe position while guiding the reversing vehicle;

- if necessary, high visibility clothing is provided for and worn by banksmen;

- training in the use of recognised signals is given to drivers and anyone who controls vehicle movements;

- floors and roadways are kept in good condition.

For further information see the free leaflet *Managing vehicle safety at the workplace* (INDG199).

Loading and unloading of vehicles

Accidents frequently happen when people fall from vehicles, or the load moves unexpectedly and they are struck by it. Particular dangers exist where reels of paper are being unloaded as they are heavy and gain momentum once they start to move.

Unloading of reels needs to be done with suitable equipment such as a clamp, boom or pole attachment on a lift truck, and with a safe system of work. Tilting clamp devices are particularly useful, as they permit reels to be picked up from the horizontal and placed vertically, or vice versa.

A reputable supplier of lift truck attachments will be able to give advice about suitable equipment for your job, and the effect the use of the device will have on the rated capacity of your truck.

Points to check include:

- the need to climb on loads is avoided, by using curtain-sided vehicles, or proprietary sheeting systems;

- safe access is provided if work must be done at a height;

- safety lines and harnesses are provided and worn if walking on high loads cannot be avoided;

- manual unloading of reels is eliminated if at all possible;

- people keep well clear of the area during loading and unloading operations;

- manual handling is avoided by use of pallet, lift truck or a porter's trolley;

- a safe system is devised to deal with mishaps, such as stuck loads. A common mistake is to attempt to free a stuck load by tying a rope to it and pulling with the lift truck, injuries occur when the rope or its fixing breaks and it recoils violently;

- instructions exist for dealing with any vehicle that might arrive on-site with an unsafe load, and that they are observed;

- arrangements are made to adequately secure loads before vehicles leave the site, an example is the need to secure loads inside curtain-sided vehicles, to prevent dangerous movement of the load in transit.

Racking should be securely fixed and have aisles wide enough to allow manoeuvring

Safe stacking and storing

General principles

- Storage areas should be specifically designated, clearly marked and in the charge of a responsible person.

- Consider permissible floor loadings.

- Place materials handled by crane or lift truck on battens or other suitable material to ensure that a sling or forks can be inserted under them.

- Good housekeeping is essential at all times.

- Provide adequate lighting.

- Maintain adequate clearance between rows to ensure safe stacking and withdrawal.

- Position loads capable of being stacked directly on top of each other on a firm, level base.

- Check stacks periodically for stability and take corrective measures where necessary.

- Consider fire precautions at an early stage, stacks which are too high may prevent sprinkler systems from working correctly.

Don't:

- exceed the safe load of racks, shelves or floors;

- allow items to stick out from stacks into gangways;

- climb racks to reach upper shelves - use a ladder or steps;

- lean heavy stacks against walls;

- de-stack by throwing down from the top or pulling out from the bottom.

Racking installations

Racking should:

- be installed and maintained in accordance with the manufacturer's instructions;

- be erected on sound, level floors capable of withstanding the point loading of each base plate;

- be securely fixed to the floor where lift trucks and mechanical handling equipment are used. If racks have to be secured to the building, calculations should confirm the building is satisfactory for this purpose;

- have aisles wide enough to ensure that mechanical handling equipment can be easily manoeuvred;

- have the maximum load clearly stated on them;

- never be altered without consulting the manufacturer first;

- have high visibility for key components to assist lift truck drivers to position their forks correctly.

Use of pallets

Operators should receive instruction on the safe use of pallets. Accidents involving pallets are caused by:

- poor design;

- poor construction;

- use of pallets unsuitable for particular loads/racking systems;

- continued use of damaged pallets;

- bad handling.

Precautions to reduce the risk of accidents:

- An effective pallet damage inspection scheme should be established at the goods-in stage. If pallets are regularly in a damaged condition, take action with the supplier.

- All pallets should be inspected again each time before re-use (damaged ones should be withdrawn).

- Empty pallets should be carefully handled and not dragged or thrown about.

- To avoid damage to pallets, and to lift the loads safely, the forks of any handling device should extend into the pallet to at least three-quarters of its depth.

- Forks should not extend beyond the pallet being lifted (eg they could overturn an adjacent load).

- As a general guide, the height of the load should not exceed the longest base dimension of the pallet.

- Stacking of palletised loads capable of being crushed should be avoided.

Reel storage and stacking

Ideally, pedestrians should be excluded from reel storage areas in which lift trucks are used. This is especially important when stacking or de-stacking operations are being performed.

Stacking reels on end often requires the use of clamp trucks or similar equipment. The maximum height for any stack will depend on the reel size and will be limited by stability, driver vision and overhead obstructions. There should be good lighting with minimum shadow. Reels should be stacked safely. Pillars should be clearly marked, eg with yellow banding.

Where clamp trucks or other safe means of stacking on end are not available, reels will probably be stored horizontally. It is safest to store reels without stacking but if they are stacked more than one tier high due to lack of space, it is vital to use proper wedges to prevent accidental breaking down of the stack. If wedges are too small or incorrectly shaped, not only will they be liable to move, but the paper will also be damaged. At least one wedge should be placed at each side of every reel at floor level - large wedges with handles may be best.

Stacking aisles should be of sufficient width for any vehicles undertaking the work.

Further advice on all reel stacking methods is given in the publication *Handling reels of paper and board*.

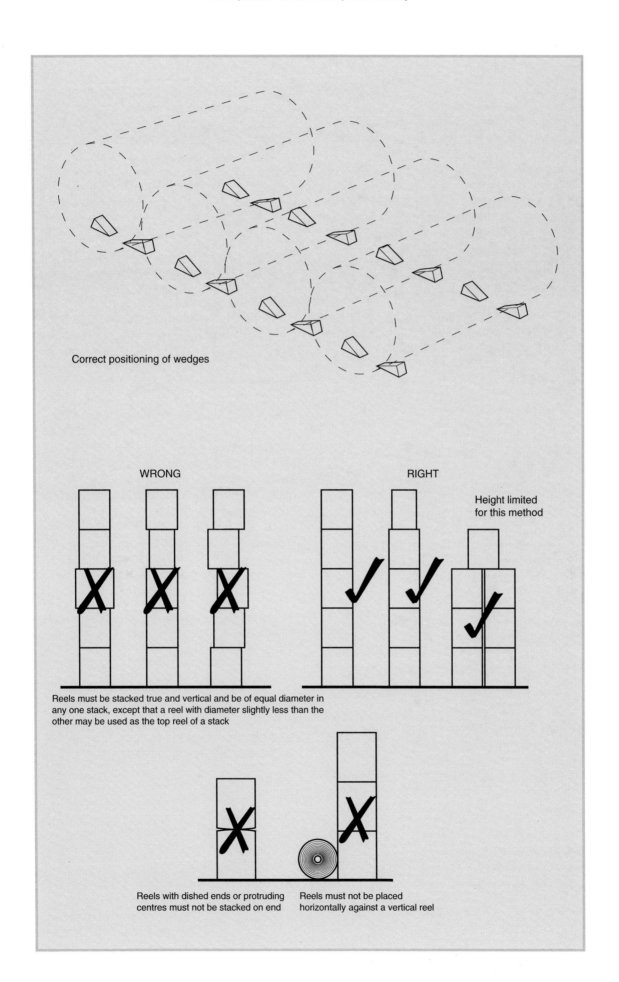

Correct positioning of wedges

WRONG

RIGHT

Height limited
for this method

Reels must be stacked true and vertical and be of equal diameter in
any one stack, except that a reel with diameter slightly less than the
other may be used as the top reel of a stack

Reels with dished ends or protruding
centres must not be stacked on end

Reels must not be placed
horizontally against a vertical reel

Manual breaking down of pyramid stacks

Reels may be delivered on lorries in pyramid stacks, or be stored that way in the warehouse. Where possible, you should consider changing the delivery and storage arrangements so reels are stored and delivered on end. It is best to use mechanical methods of handling reels stacked like this, for example by using a lift truck with tilting clamp, lifting boom or tine devices - ask a specialist supplier of lift truck attachments for advice. Mechanical handling devices will help to protect your employees and also help to prevent damage to the reels.

If manual breaking down of such stacks cannot be eliminated, a safe system of work must be set down and implemented. The system needs to take account of the following:

- the need to de-stack reels in a pre-determined order;

- the need to ensure that people only work from the side of the stack, where they will not be hit by a reel if it moves suddenly;

- the need to adequately and firmly chock all reels on the bottom row of the stack until it is necessary to move them (chock design is important - the height of the chock should be at least one eighth of the diameter of the reel);

- the use of properly designed bats or paddles to control unchocked reels. Braking chocks may be used, together with a chock paddle and a lever bat;

- the need to provide sufficient people for the job - unloading should be conducted by a team of at least three adequately trained and supervised people, and this may include the driver of the delivery lorry. One person will drive the lift truck, while the other two work at the side of the stack, barring down the reels.

Fatal accidents have occurred when reels being manually de-stacked have run out of control - mechanical methods should be used if at all possible.

Lift and clamp trucks

Lift and clamp trucks can be used for many material handling operations in the printing industry, particularly in the movement of pallets of paper, paper reels, chemicals and waste materials. Lift truck accidents cause many serious injuries including fatalities every year - suitable operator training, vehicle maintenance and working conditions are essential.

The law and lift trucks

In addition to the general requirements of the Health and Safety at Work etc Act 1974 (HSWA), thorough examination and testing of the chains of a lift truck by a competent person is required. You will need to obtain and keep a copy of these reports and rectify safety deficiencies identified in them.

The publication *Rider-operated lift trucks: operator training. Approved Code of Practice and supplementary guidance* (COP 26) gives practical guidance on complying with the requirements of section 2 of the HSWA in relation to the basic training of operators of rider-operated lift trucks.

The Approved Code of Practice requires:

- employers to provide basic training for operators by recognised instructors;

- competence testing of lift truck operators;

- authorisation of, and appropriate records for, all employees permitted to drive lift trucks.

In addition to the above, driver-operated lift trucks used regularly on the road for long periods, and their drivers, must be licensed by the Department of Transport.

Health problems

Lift trucks can create ill-health problems which will need to be considered. These can include:

- breathing problems arising from the use of diesel trucks in confined working environments (good maintenance, eg of fuel injectors can reduce fume problems);

Use mechanical methods such as a clamp truck to de-stack and move reels

COMMON ACCIDENTS

Some common causes of lift truck accidents include:

- unsafe reversing;

- speeding;

- overloading;

- passenger carrying;

- untrained drivers;

- poor working environment, eg uneven road surfaces or obstacles;

- inadequate separation of pedestrians and lift trucks;

- inadequate separation of highway vehicles and lift trucks;

- poor truck maintenance including maintenance of chains and brakes.

- back and upper limb disorders due to poor seating and/or controls.

Poor roadways can cause excessive truck vibration and back problems.

Safety guidelines for lift trucks

- Ensure all operators have received adequate training.

- Ensure enough people have been trained to cover holidays, weekends, overtime and sickness.

- Ensure training instructors have undergone appropriate training in instructional techniques and skills assessment.

- Restrict use of lift trucks to authorised operators only (authorisation should only be given to adequately trained and experienced operators).

- Provide suitable refresher training for operators.

- Ensure managers and supervisors are trained in safety aspects of lift and clamp trucks.

- Managers should have an appreciation of the risks and the ways to minimise the risks.

- Supervisors should have sufficient knowledge to be able to recognise inadequacies in the operation of lift trucks and the training needs of operators.

- Screen operators for fitness, eg eyesight testing.

- Keep floors and roadways in good condition, free from obstacles, obstructions and pot holes.

- Allow adequate room for lift truck manoeuvres.

- Maintain all lift trucks on a regular basis to ensure they are in good condition (including examination of the mast chains, tyres, brakes and horns).

- Ensure that thorough examination and testing of lifting chains are being carried out by a competent person as required.

- Segregate lift truck routes from pedestrian and working areas as much as possible and mark them with barriers or lines on the floor.

- Ensure gradients are not too steep.

- Keep keys safe when the lift trucks are not being used by authorised drivers.

- Ensure good visibility when moving loads, where necessary use a banksman to direct traffic safely.

- Remember that the fitting of crane jib attachments is subject to additional legal requirements.

Don't:

- allow anyone to drive a lift truck unless they have been selected, trained and authorised to do so;

- carry reels stacked on top of each other (as the top reels will be unsupported and liable to fall);

- use lift trucks in areas where flammable concentrations of vapours may be present, eg close to gravure or flexo presses using highly flammable liquids or in ink stores unless the trucks have been specially designed and protected;

- leave keys in the ignition when trucks are parked or left unsupervised;

- allow any operators to consume any alcohol while at work;

- use forks, pallets or bins to lift persons to work at heights (use properly designed mobile work platforms);

- pick up loads if someone is standing close to the load;

- allow people to walk under raised loads;

- move unstable loads;

- leave a lift truck unattended on a gradient except in an emergency (if you do have to leave the truck on a slope in an emergency use wheel chocks);

- carry passengers unless the lift truck is designed to do so;

- run over cables or flexible pipes on the floor unless they are suitably protected;

- operate with the load raised except for stacking and de-stacking manoeuvres;

- allow speeding or unsafe reversing practices;

- fit attachments to lift trucks which could affect their lifting capacity without consulting the manufacturer, authorised supplier or qualified lift truck engineer;

- use lift trucks without suitable lighting;

- forget to consider needs for beacons, mirrors, horns, seatbelts etc and the protection of drivers from falling objects;

- allow other people, such as delivery drivers, to use your lift trucks unless you are certain that they have received appropriate training etc.

Safety guidelines for automatic guided vehicles (AGVs)

These include:

- ensuring that all safety features are operating correctly;

- ensuring that stopping performances are appropriate to the risk and load. Vehicles will need to come to a controlled stop so as not to release their load suddenly;

- ensuring that appropriate maximum speeds are set;

- ensuring that adequate clearances have been left to prevent trapping people between moving vehicles and fixed structures.

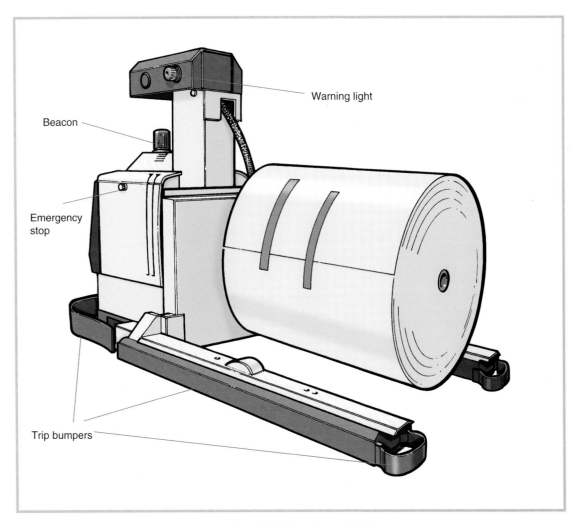

Diagram of an AGV showing safety features

WARNING CONTAINS ASBESTOS

Breathing asbestos dust is dangerous to health

Follow safety instructions

Asbestos in buildings

Asbestos related diseases kill an estimated 3000 people each year in the UK and the figure is expected to rise. Many of the people now suffering from these diseases worked in the building and maintenance trades - joiners, plumbers, electricians, engineers etc.

As a rough guide, if your building was built before the 1980s and you carry out any type of maintenance, repair or refurbishment work, you could be exposing people to asbestos dust without realising it. Any individual exposure may be small but these can build up and may result in an asbestos related disease later on in life. This is particularly relevant to maintenance personnel.

Where is asbestos found in buildings?

The following are areas where asbestos might be found in older buildings:

- in spray coating for fire protection and insulation on steelwork, concrete walls and ceilings;

- in insulation lagging, on pipework, and for boilers and ducts;

- in asbestos insulating board used as wall partitions, fire doors, ceiling tiles etc;

- in asbestos cement products such as sheeting on walls and roofs, tiles, cold water tanks, gutters, pipes and in decorative plaster finishes.

What should you do?

- Identify any asbestos material on site (if you are unsure, have it tested). Keep a record of its location.

- Ensure any relevant employees or contractors know if and where asbestos may be present within your works.

- Ensure any asbestos you do find is in a safe condition, eg undamaged and/or sealed (and will not affect existing employees working in your factory). Carry out regular checks to make sure that it remains safe.

- If work is required on or near the asbestos you may need to call in licensed contractors. You will need to inform anyone carrying out the work of the dangers and ensure they carry out the work safely.

- Ask your local enforcing authority for further information. Free and priced publications are available, eg *Asbestos dust - the hidden killer. Are you at risk? Essential advice for building maintenance, repair and refurbishment workers* (INDG187).

Chapter 4
HEALTH RISKS

See the References section at the back of the book for details of publications which relate to HEALTH RISKS

Over 2 million people a year suffer from ill health caused or made worse by work. Thirteen million working days are lost as people take time off because work has made them ill. The printing industry is no exception. Ill-health problems include musculoskeletal disorders, occupational asthma, deafness, eye damage and dermatitis. Dermatitis is a particular problem in printing; European reports have indicated that it accounts for 65% of all cases of ill health in the industry.

The management of health risks within the workplace is often neglected or fails because, unlike safety issues, health risks tend to be both less obvious and less well understood. Because the onset of ill health is often delayed the risks can be under-estimated until it is too late and permanent damage has occurred.

Employers have just as much responsibility for safeguarding the health as the safety of their employees. Risk assessments need to cover health as well as safety hazards, see the general advice given on risk assessment in Chapter 1.

Relevant legislation

Relevant legislation on health risks includes:

- The Health and Safety at Work etc Act 1974

- The Control of Substances Hazardous to Health (COSHH) Regulations 1994

- The Management of Health and Safety at Work Regulations 1992

- The Workplace (Health, Safety and Welfare) Regulations 1992

- The Noise at Work Regulations 1989

- The Control of Lead at Work Regulations 1980 (CLAW)

- Manual Handling Operations Regulations 1992

- The Control of Asbestos at Work Regulations 1987

- The Ionising Radiations Regulations 1985

Table 1 Examples of health hazards in printing

Hazard	Health effects	Typical processes
Inhalation of solvent vapour (health effects depend on the solvent, its concentration in air and the length of exposure) Contact with and absorption of solvent through the skin	Headaches, nausea Effects on the central nervous system Liver and kidney damage Dermatitis	Cleaning litho and letterpress rollers and cylinders Screen, flexo and gravure printing
Inhalation of vapours and mists from isocyanates or reactive acrylates	Occupational asthma	Use of lacquers, adhesives, inks etc containing isocyanates or reactive acrylates
Skin contact with reactive chemicals (health effects depend on the chemical, its concentration and the length of exposure)	Dermatitis including sensitisation (skin allergy)	Use of UV cured products Etching, engraving Platemaking Screen reclamation Stereo roller preparation Gravure cylinder preparation
Exposure to high levels of noise	Noise-induced deafness Tinnitus	Web printing Print finishing
Unsafe manual handling Awkward or repetitive movements	Back injuries Upper limb disorders, eg tenosynovitis and carpal tunnel syndrome	Handling of paper reels and sheets Typesetting Print finishing
Exposure to micro-organisms from contaminated water	Humidifier fever Legionnaires' disease	Paper storage or printing where humidifiers are used Any printing process in buildings with cooling towers or other water systems that can become contaminated

The use of hazardous substances at work is subject to the COSHH Regulations

Hazardous substances

Many chemical substances can cause harm if they are inhaled or they are absorbed through the skin. Many also cause dermatitis or damage to the eyes. Exposure can have an immediate effect or may be delayed. Repeated exposure to some substances may cause damage to the lungs, liver or other organs. They can be taken into the body by breathing them in, passing through the skin or by eating or drinking contaminated food.

Some substances can cause both local and internal effects, for example they might damage the skin and cause liver damage. The most effective way to protect employees from any harmful substance is to see if the use of the substance can be avoided completely, perhaps by finding a safer substitute or by changing the process in some way.

Many of the health hazards listed in Table 1 relate to the use of hazardous substances. With the exceptions of asbestos and lead (for which there are specialised regulations), the use of hazardous substances at work is subject to the

Control of Substances Hazardous to Health (COSHH) Regulations 1994. This section summarises the requirements of COSHH and gives advice on the control measures for particular printing processes which involve the use of hazardous substances.

Under COSHH you must:

- assess the risks to health arising from the use of hazardous substances at work (and review your assessment if changes occur);

- prevent or control the risk, for example by using a safer substitute, or by suitable control measures;

- ensure that control measures are used and maintained;

- monitor exposure and carry out health surveillance when necessary;

- inform, instruct and train your employees about the risks and the precautions needed;

- keep records where required.

Assessment under COSHH

First gather information on the substances used in your workplace. Use manufacturers' labels and safety data sheets to help you decide which ones are hazardous. Any substance which carries the classification 'very toxic', 'toxic', 'harmful', 'corrosive', or 'irritant', or which has been assigned a maximum exposure limit (MEL) or occupational exposure standard (OES), is subject to the COSHH Regulations. This also applies to biological agents, substantial quantities of dusts and other substances which present comparable hazards.

Suppliers of chemicals for use at work are legally obliged to provide safety data sheets containing information under 16 headings, specified in the Chemicals (Hazardous Information and Packaging) (CHIP) Regulations. This information will help you to carry out your assessment, but simply collecting information is not enough - you need to use the information to decide whether or not there is a risk, and whether or not your own controls and working procedures are sufficient.

Contact your supplier for advice if you are in any doubt. See also the free leaflet *Supply of chemicals to printers - health and safety information* and the booklet *Chemical safety in the printing industry* for more detailed guidance.

Consider:

- how the substance is used, handled or stored;

- who might be affected;

- the likely routes of exposure - inhalation, ingestion, skin absorption;

- the likelihood and effects of spills or leaks;

- what control measures are currently used;

- any risks during cleaning or maintenance activities.

It is important to find out how substances are actually used in the workplace, and who is exposed to them - don't forget contractors and maintenance workers. Follow the journey substances take from delivery, to use and disposal. Think also about what can go wrong, for example how you would deal with spillage or leaking containers of solvent, or carry out repairs on machines where there is uncured UV ink. Draw conclusions about the risks and decide if you need to take action to reduce them. Specialist help may be required to help you make these decisions, for example from an occupational health specialist. Record your conclusions.

The use of safety data sheets

Labels and safety data sheets supplied with dangerous chemicals do not constitute a COSHH assessment on their own but they do contain important information about hazards to help you carry out COSHH assessments and use the chemicals safely.

The information in a safety data sheet tells the user what hazards a product or substance may have, and what precautions need to be taken so that it is used safely and without risk to health. By law, safety data sheets must contain 16 specified headings, following the steps below will help to make sense of the detail provided in some of the sections.

Step 1

Look at the section headed 'Regulatory information'. This will indicate if the product is harmful to health, and will indicate the main hazards by which the product has been classified by the supplier. If there is no hazard classification in this section you will still need to take care in assessing the use of the product, because it may be used in a process or manner that could give rise to risk.

Step 2

Look at the sections headed 'Composition', 'Hazards identification', 'Physical and chemical properties' and 'Toxicological information' to find out what in the product is harmful, and the hazards and health effects posed. For example, look for products with occupational

exposure limits, these are expressed as occupational exposure standards (OESs) or maximum exposure limits (MELs). Remember that substances with low occupational exposure limits will generally be potentially more hazardous than those with higher limits. Remember also that occupational exposure limits relate to airborne concentrations of the substance: many materials, such as press cleaning agents, are also harmful to the skin.

Step 3

Review the information in the sections 'Handling and storage', 'Stability and reactivity', 'Exposure controls/personal protection', 'Disposal considerations' and 'Ecological information', and compare it to your own work procedures. Look at storage, handling and all aspects of the job, including maintenance activities where these may result in exposure to the product. Examples of the latter are where work may be carried out on a press at which there may be uncured ink containing acrylates, or where breakdown work is needed at a heated dryer on a laminating unit in which there is adhesive containing isocyanates. Consider what precautions are taken and whether these are enough.

Step 4

Review the 'First aid', 'Fire fighting' and 'Accidental release' sections against your own company procedures to check that adequate emergency procedures are in place.

Prevention or control of exposure

If your assessment concludes that there are risks to health, then you need to decide what else you need to do to comply with the COSHH Regulations.

If possible, prevent the exposure by using a less hazardous substance or a different

process. For example, replace or eliminate volatile organic compounds in the process, by changing the blanket wash or taking steps to reduce or eliminate isopropylalcohol (IPA) from the fount solution. Ask your supplier if safer alternatives are available for the products you use.

Where prevention is not possible, you need

to consider control measures. This usually means a combination of some of the following:

- Enclosing the process.

- Partial enclosure and/or local exhaust ventilation (LEV).

- General ventilation.

- Systems of work and handling procedures to minimise leaks and spills.

- If, and only if, you cannot adequately control exposure by a combination of the measures above, then you should also provide personal protective equipment (PPE) such as respiratory protective equipment, gloves and eye protection. See the section on 'Personal protective equipment (PPE)' towards the end of this chapter for further information.

Exposure limits

For certain substances, where there is a risk to health through inhalation, occupational exposure limits have been set. There are two kinds - maximum exposure limits (MELs) and occupational exposure standards (OESs). Both types of limit are concentrations of hazardous substances in the air, averaged over a specified period of time. The occupational exposure limit value should be compared with exposure levels in the workplace, to see whether exposure to the substance is being properly controlled. Air monitoring may be necessary under COSHH. You may need advice about this from an occupational hygienist.

Further information and an explanation of the difference between the two types of exposure limits is given in HSE guidance note *Occupational Exposure Limits* (EH40).

Make sure that controls are kept in good order and that employees know how to use them properly. See the section in this chapter on 'Local exhaust ventilation' for more detailed advice on its design, use and maintenance. Consider whether monitoring of exposure is required to check that control measures are effective.

See the section on 'Other health issues' later in this chapter for detailed advice on health surveillance.

Make sure that employees are properly instructed on the risks of the substances used in their work, and that they are properly trained to use any safety equipment including personal protective equipment. Ensure that they know how to report defects, and to recognise and report any adverse health effects.

Chemical hazards in printing

Table 2 Printing processes which may give rise to skin or eye contact hazards

Process or activity	Type/name of substance	Potential health hazard
Etching, engraving, platemaking, certain photographic reproduction systems, correction of litho plates (hydrofluoric acid)	Corrosive acids, eg concentrated nitric and sulphuric acids, hydrofluoric acid	Skin burns and blisters Burns with concentrated hydrofluoric acid are very severe Eye damage
Cleaning of screens in screen printing	Strong alkalis, eg concentrated sodium or potassium hydroxide	Corrosive to skin, eyes and mucous membrane

Table 2 Printing processes which may give rise to skin or eye contact hazards (continued)

Process or activity	Type/name of substance	Potential health hazard
Concentrated photographic developer solutions	Hydroquinone	Irritant to eyes but may cause permanent damage Irritant and sensitising to the skin, may cause dermatitis
UV and electron beam curable inks, varnishes and lacquers	Reactive acrylates or methacrylates	Corrosive to skin, eyes and mucous membranes Potential for skin sensitisation
Photographic fixer solutions	Acetic acid, acidic salt solutions (eg sodium thiosulphate)	Irritant
Hardener added to photographic fixer solutions	Dilute formaldehyde solution	Irritant Frequent contact may lead to skin sensitisation
Litho platemaking, gravure cylinder preparation, photo-engraving, photographic bleaches	Dichromates, eg ammonium, potassium and sodium dichromates	Very corrosive In high concentrations can cause deep ulcers Potential for skin sensitisation
Litho printing: fount solution, blanket restorers, cleaning solvents	Isopropylalcohol (IPA), methyl ethyl ketone (MEK), white spirit	Dermatitis
Gravure and flexographic printing: various inks	MEK Alcohols, eg industrial methylated spirits (IMS), IPA Esters, eg ethyl acetate Aromatic hydrocarbons, eg toluene, xylene	Dermatitis
Screen printing: inks	Ketones, eg cyclohexanone Aromatic hydrocarbons, eg xylene	Dermatitis

Note: The examples here are only illustrative and are not exhaustive

Table 3 Printing processes which may give rise to inhalation hazards

Examples of process or activity	Type/name of substance	Potential health hazard
Cleaning rollers, cylinders and blanket restoring	Chlorinated hydrocarbons, eg perchloroethylene Ketones, eg methyl ethyl ketone (MEK)	Dizziness, drowsiness and other effects on the central nervous system Cardiac arrhythmia (high concentration) Affects liver and kidneys on long-term exposure
Litho printing - fount solution	Alcohols such as isopropylalcohol (IPA)	Dizziness, drowsiness and other effects on the central nervous system
Gravure and flexographic printing	Inks containing ketones (eg cyclohexanone), alcohols (as in IMS), esters (eg ethyl acetate, isopropyl acetate) or aromatic hydrocarbons, eg toluene, xylene	As above
Screen printing	Inks containing ketones or aromatic hydrocarbons	As above
Adhesive laminating Use of polyurethane lacquers	Isocyanate prepolymers	Irritation of respiratory tract (high concentration) Occupational asthma could occur even at low levels
Handling, cutting, grinding lead type, hot metal work	Lead dust/fume	Lead absorbed in bloodstream leads to headaches, tiredness, stomach pains, constipation and loss of weight
Dyeline printing	Ammonium hydroxide	Irritation of respiratory tract (as ammonia vapour)
High speed printing using UV ink - leading to ink misting	Reactive acrylates contained in UV inks etc	Irritation of respiratory tract Potential for occupational asthma
Laser engraving (gravure cylinders)	Metal fume	Irritation of respiratory tract, 'flu-like' illness (metal fume fever depending on the metal)
Maintenance involving welding		Poisoning from substances in the fume

Table 3 Printing processes which may give rise to inhalation hazards (continued)

Examples of process or activity	Type/name of substance	Potential health hazard
Use of UV lamps for photo processing, UV curing, corona discharge	Ozone	Irritation of upper respiratory tract Headaches and nausea
Dusts		
Saw/knife milling in bindery	Paper	
Use of anti-set-off powder	Sugar/starch	
Thermography	Plasticisers	Dust of any kind can irritate the respiratory tract and block the nose
Bronzing machines, mixing aluminium pastes	Metal	
Manufacture of formes	Softwood dust	Respiratory disorders including occupational asthma
Maintenance involving cutting, sawing, drilling etc	Hardwood	Occupational asthma and cancers
Maintenance work, particularly to buildings	Asbestos (see last section of Chapter 3)	Cancers and asbestosis

Specific process health hazards

Design and art work

Risks to health from design and art work can be reduced by:

- using non-flammable adhesives - preferably wax;

- removing wax from glass surfaces by scraping and not with solvent;

- only using aerosols if there is good ventilation;

- not smoking where aerosols are used - many will be flammable;

- if an alternative to an aerosol is available - use it.

Graphic reproduction

Darkrooms with automatic film processors need mechanical ventilation to ensure healthy and comfortable working conditions. Ten to fifteen air changes per hour is the standard normally achieved in the industry. A suitable extractor fan mounted in an outside wall will do, but it is important to provide an air inlet. Carefully designed louvre covers will ensure that unwanted light does not enter the room.

Platemaking

Automatic processing effectively reduces the likelihood of skin contact with chemicals during normal operation. Some developers can cause aggressive skin reactions, so nitrile or butyl rubber gauntlets and protective clothing are needed when manipulating the

Use drip trays and automatic pumping to reduce skin contact with chemicals

chemical containers. Suitable goggles or face shields should be provided and worn if there is a risk of splashing.

Keep drums of replenisher solution feeding process equipment in shallow trays, so as to contain spillage (and protect the floor).

Deletion fluids containing hydrofluoric acid in toxic and corrosive concentrations may be used to make minor alterations to printing plates. These products are particularly harmful if skin or eye contact occurs - the affected area should be washed immediately under running water, and medical advice obtained.

Check the safety data sheets for these products to ensure that appropriate first aid is available. Antidote cream (calcium gluconate gel) will prevent serious burns right down to the bone. If it is needed, keep fresh stock on the premises. Make sure people know why it is needed and how to use it.

Where possible, use deletion pens as an alternative to small jars or pots of deletion fluid to reduce the danger of skin contact.

If large scale deletion work is essential, keep the containers of deletion fluids in secure storage when not in use.

Lithographic printing

Wash-up solvents have commonly included white spirit and similar mixtures of petroleum distillates. Vegetable oil derivatives are now available for use as roller cleaners, and these products usually reduce risk to health by inhalation. Skin contact may remain a problem so that a skin care regime may be necessary. Try using these products as part of the substitution approach under COSHH.

Other more volatile and aggressive organic solvents found include those used for removal of dried ink or to swell low areas of the blanket. Check with the suppliers to see if the least hazardous product has been chosen. Whatever solvent is selected, set out a safe system of work to control its use and reduce exposure. Use of these products should be kept to a minimum.

Humidifiers may be used to maintain suitable environmental conditions for litho printing. (See under 'Humidifier fever' in the 'Other health issues' section later in this chapter. This needs to be considered if humidifiers with water reservoirs are used.)

Ultraviolet (UV) curable materials

Particular care is needed when handling ultraviolet (UV) curable materials (inks, varnishes and lacquers). The first signs of harmful effect - reddening of the skin and a rash - may not appear until 24 hours after exposure, and will get worse over two or three days. A system of skin inspection will identify any printers who develop problems (see the section on 'Health surveillance in practice' later in this chapter).

Wash-up solvents with traces of UV curable materials are a particular danger. The solvent has a drying effect on the skin, and this enables the UV curable material to penetrate more easily. Keep such solvents off skin and clothing.

If contact does occur, wash off immediately with plenty of soap and water. Remove contaminated clothing immediately. Send it for laundering, but make sure it is properly packaged to prevent inadvertent contact and labelled, indicating the hazard, so as to protect other people who may handle it. If eyes are affected, clean with plenty of water and get medical help.

Also consider maintenance work; an engineer working on a press using UV ink was sensitised after contact with the uncured ink - suitable protective clothing including gloves would have protected him.

Screen printing and cleaning

Screen printing areas need very good ventilation to keep the air clear of fumes. Position mechanical ventilation so that it

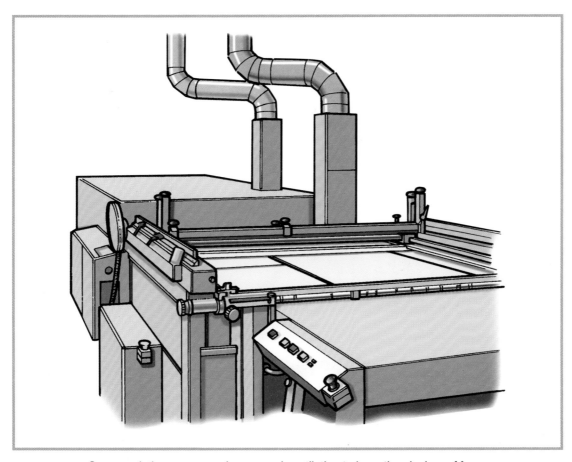

Screen printing areas need very good ventilation to keep the air clear of fumes

draws fumes away from the printers. Site the drying racks so that the airflow across them also draws the fume away from the working position. Vent drying tunnels to a safe place outside.

Screen printing inks and solvents may contain glycol-ethers and their esters. Like many other solvents, glycol ethers can cause giddiness, headaches, loss of co-ordination and nausea. Some are more hazardous than others, as they can also affect the bone-marrow and cause aplastic anaemia and ought not to be used. Avoid those containing: 2-ethoxy ethanol, 2-methoxy ethanol, 2-ethoxy ethyl acetate and 2-methoxy ethyl acetate. Check with your supplier if in doubt.

Do not use high pressure water jets to clean screens doused with solvents, as this will result in unnecessarily high levels of airborne solvent.

Clean screens in a mechanically ventilated area such as a booth. Do not jet them until they are free from ink and solvent.

Operators should wear eye protection

(goggles or visors), aprons, gloves or gauntlets and waterproof boots when using high pressure water/steam cleaners. Ventilation, electrical safety, hearing protection and drainage need to be planned when the wet cleaning area is set out. Further information is available in two publications, *Control of health hazards in screen printing* and *Electrical risks from steam/water pressure cleaners* (PM29).

Use of isocyanates

Isocyanates may be found in adhesives used in the adhesive laminating process, polyurethane lacquers, primers and certain specialised inks.

Isocyanates are respiratory sensitisers and have the potential to cause asthmatic attacks, which may occur immediately on exposure, or after a delay of several hours. Health surveillance will be necessary in most circumstances: take specialist advice from an occupational physician about this.

Try to choose products which do not contain

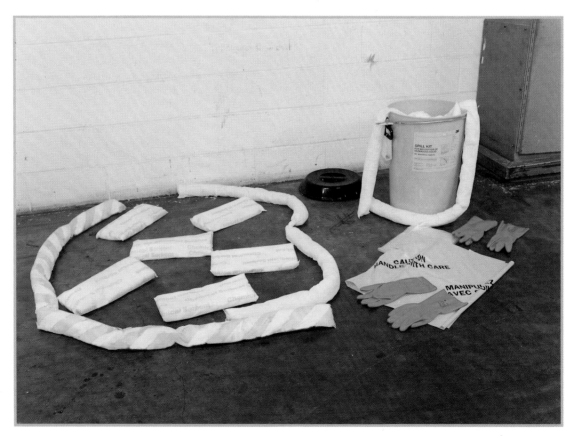

Provide facilities for dealing with spillages such as a spill kit

isocyanates if possible, but if they are unavoidable, choose those which have the minimum isocyanate content necessary to fulfil production requirements.

Care is needed to ensure that control measures are selected and implemented to prevent inhalation of isocyanates. Local exhaust ventilation will be appropriate in many situations. Risk is likely to be greater in situations in which the substance is heated, or when misting or aerosol formation may occur (the operating speed of the machine may be relevant to this).

General protective clothing, including gloves and eye protection, will be necessary, and in certain situations respiratory protective equipment will be needed - this will be determined by the COSHH assessment.

Provide facilities for first aid and for dealing with spillages, skin and eye contamination and other emergencies. See the booklet *Safe use of isocyanates in printing and laminating* for further guidance.

Disposal of waste

Remember that the disposal of waste materials and nominally empty containers are subject to environmental regulations. Take advice from the supplier and your local authority.

Noise

Loud noise at work can cause irreversible hearing damage. It accelerates the normal hearing loss which occurs as we grow older. It can cause other problems such as tinnitus (troublesome noises in the ear), interference with communication, and stress.

Civil claims against employers are common, and many are successful because not enough has been done in the past to protect the hearing of people at work.

Do you have a noise problem?

As a rule of thumb, if you cannot hear a normal conversation in your workplace clearly when you are 2 m away from the speaker, the noise level is likely to be around 85 dB(A) or higher. If you cannot hear someone clearly when you are about 1 m away, the level is likely to be around 90 dB(A) or higher.

If you think you may have a problem find out what the noise levels are in your workplace by taking measurements.

Measuring noise levels

Noise is measured in decibels - you will usually see it written as dB(A). The noise level (sound pressure) is measured logarithmically so that every 3 dB(A) increase means a doubling of the noise energy, for example 93 dB(A) is twice as hazardous as 90 dB(A).

In most jobs, the risk depends not just on the noise levels, but also how long people are exposed, including any overtime. For more information see *Sound solutions - techniques to reduce noise at work* (HSG138).

Noise and the law

The Noise at Work Regulations 1989 are intended to reduce hearing damage caused by loud noise and they lay down three action levels. The Regulations require employers to assess the risks and take action when workers' daily exposure to noise reaches the 85 dB(A) $(L_{EP,d})$* 'first action level' and further action if it reaches

* Daily personal noise exposure: the worker's noise exposure averaged over an eight-hour working period.

Do you have a noise problem? Loud noise at work can cause irreversible hearing damage

the 90 dB(A) ($L_{EP,d}$) second or 140 dB(A) 'peak' action levels. When measuring noise exposure no account is taken of the effect of any personal ear protectors worn.

If you find that the noise level is at the first action level or above you must:

- have the risk assessed by a competent person;

- tell your workers about the risks and precautions;

- make hearing protection freely available to those who want it where levels exceed 85 dB(A).

If you find that the noise levels are at the second action level or above, in addition to the above actions, you must also:

- do all that is reasonably practicable to reduce exposure without relying on hearing protection, eg use engineering controls;

- use recognised safety signs to identify and restrict entry to zones where noise reaches (or exceeds) the second or peak action levels. Employees, including managers and supervisors, must not enter these zones unless wearing suitable and effective hearing protection.

Noise reduction

Consider:

- choosing quiet machines or processes for new work. Makers must reduce noise by good design and construction and also provide noise data with their equipment if levels are likely to reach or exceed the first action level. If you are buying machinery, insist on this information. Once the machinery is installed, check the noise levels and take any steps necessary to reduce noise. Noise emission levels can be limited as part of the contract with suppliers and checked after installation;

- changing the machine and process to produce less noise. Don't forget that other changes you make might affect noise levels;

- enclosing noisy machines by providing acoustic enclosures. These have to be made of appropriate noise-reducing materials and correctly installed. If they are not properly designed, noise escaping from holes, feed openings or poorly fitting panels may significantly reduce performance. Specialist advice will probably be necessary;

- putting noisy machines and processes in separate rooms, away from employees' work areas;

- fitting silencers to all exhausts and making sure they are kept in place and maintained.

Reducing exposure

- Think about reducing the length of exposure by rotating jobs or providing a noise refuge, eg at machine control points.

- Remember - hearing damage is cumulative. Make sure that young people in particular get into the habit of avoiding noise exposure, before their hearing is permanently damaged.

Providing hearing protection

Ensure that workers wear hearing protection where daily personal noise levels exceed 90 dB(A). Remember this is not a substitute for noise reduction at source.

Do not rely too heavily on hearing protectors. In practice they reduce noise exposure less than is claimed because they:

- have not been correctly selected;

- are not fitted/worn correctly;

- are not properly maintained;

- are uncomfortable or inconvenient to wear.

Plastic foam or mineral fibre/waxed plugs, if properly chosen and correctly worn, can be as good as ear muffs. To work, hearing protectors need to be worn all the time that people are in noisy areas. If they are left off for even short periods, even the best protectors cannot greatly reduce noise exposure. Supervision should check this.

It will be beneficial for employees to have a choice of hearing protection from a range of types identified as suitable.

It is good practice to carry out regular hearing checks on all employees whose daily personal noise exposures equal or exceed 90 dB(A), and such checks should be carried out when noise levels reach or exceed 95 dB(A). Refer to the leaflet *Health surveillance in noisy industries* (INDG193) and the paragraphs under 'Hearing protection' in the 'Personal protective equipment (PPE)' section at the end of this chapter.

Workers need to be adequately trained in the proper fitting, use and care or hearing protection. This will help to ensure that protectors maintain their efficiency and are correctly worn.

Common problems and solutions for printers

Experience has shown that there are certain areas that can usefully be targeted in order to reduce noise in a printers.

- Sheet-fed buckle-folding machines in the finishing department create high noise levels. These machines should be fitted with acoustic hoods at all buckle plates to reduce the noise. Guidance is given in the publication *Noise reduction at buckle-folding machines*.

- Web-fed presses have several noise sources (a main one being the folder), and various noise control measures may be appropriate. Guidance is contained in the booklet *Noise reduction at web-fed presses*.

- Vacuum pumps and compressors, such as those associated with sheet-fed printing machines, gatherer-stitcher-trimmers and buckle-folding machines, can produce high noise levels and it is important to site such equipment away from the workroom as these can make a large contribution to the overall noise level.

- Sheet-fed printing machines (in general) do not create excessive levels of noise if they are properly spaced and housed, provided that noise from vacuum pumps and compressors is controlled.

- Regular preventive maintenance of machines can be important in avoiding the generation of excessive levels of noise. Worn bearings in buckle-folding machines are frequently found to be a significant source of noise.

Manual handling

The law and manual handling

The Manual Handling Operations Regulations 1992 require all employers to:

- avoid the need for hazardous manual lifting and handling if it is reasonably practicable to do so, eg by redesigning the task and/or workplace layout, eliminating the need to move loads manually, using mechanical handling equipment etc;

- assess the risk of injury from any hazardous manual lifting and handling which cannot be avoided;

- take steps to reduce the risk of injury from manual handling, eg by providing mechanical assistance, improvements to the task, load or working environment;

- provide employees with information on the weight of the load and an indication of the heaviest side where a load has a centre of gravity that is not centrally positioned.

What are the risks?

Although some people are more at risk, everyone can suffer injuries as a result of manual handling - this is why hazardous manual handling activities should be avoided if possible. If it is impossible to avoid such activity then it should be assessed and risk reduction measures considered. When making an assessment, you may have to give particular attention to the following groups of people:

- younger, more inexperienced employees;

- older and/or less physically fit employees;

- those with existing injuries;

- pregnant employees.

Manual/materials handling can lead to injuries and musculoskeletal disorders in various parts of the body including the back, abdomen, neck, upper limbs and even lower limbs.

The cumulative effects of even minor injuries can become more pronounced over a period of time. Serious and lasting damage to the spine and other parts of the body can result. Careful job design can avoid the problems of restricting particular tasks to particular workers or the disruption that can follow if people are injured.

Reel and cylinder trolleys reduce the amount of manual lifting and carrying

Poor lifting and carrying, pushing and pulling causes more than 25% of the work-related injuries reported in the printing industry each year.

Reducing the risks

When manual handling is unavoidable, look at the job and think about reducing the risk by providing mechanical help, for example:

- scissor lifts and elevating tables at folders and guillotines;

- pile turners and joggers to reduce the need for hand turning and 'knocking up';

- mechanical or free-running conveyors to reduce lifting and carrying;

- hoists and slings at reelstands to reduce manual lifting of paper reels, especially those mounted on swing arms;

- reel conveyor trolleys for localised movement of paper reels into and out of reelstands;

- cylinder and roller trolleys;

- sack trucks.

Other ways of reducing the risk include:

- making the load smaller/lighter or easier to grasp, eg by buying in smaller paper bundles or chemical containers;

- reorganising or redesigning the tasks to reduce the effort required;

- altering workstation heights to suit the worker;

- improving the layout of the workplace to make the work more efficient;

- ensuring reasonable working temperatures;

- ensuring adequate manoeuvring space has been provided etc.

ACCIDENTS

A printer lifting a magazine bundle weighing 12 kg onto a pallet injured his lower back. He had not been given any handling aids or training in correct lifting techniques.

An employee attempting to clear a jammed newspaper bundle on a conveyor injured her back. She had not been given any training or information on manual handling techniques or bundle clearing techniques.

A maintenance fitter suffered back pain after lifting press inking rollers weighing 23 kg. He had received no training or information on manual handling. Use of mechanical lifting equipment or assistance from a second person would have reduced the risk of injury.

Training

Consider providing every employee with basic training in manual handling techniques appropriate to the type of work they do. You will also have to consider other more direct ways to reduce risk. Training should cover:

- how manual handling can cause injury;

- the essentials of the Manual Handling Operations Regulations 1992;

- how to recognise potentially harmful manual handling tasks/operations;

- appropriate systems of work;

- correct use of mechanical aids;

- appropriate handling techniques.

Further information on manual handling can be found in the booklet *Manual handling. Manual Handling Operations Regulations 1992. Guidance on regulations* (L23).

Assessing and reducing risks

Job

Does the job require:

- lifting or lowering too far?
- rushing?
- carrying over long distances?
- lots of repetitions?
- twisting and turning?

Work area

Is the work area:

- too dark?
- too slippery?
- too congested/ obstructed?

Load

Is the load:

- too heavy?
- too large?
- too unstable?
- too sharp?
- too difficult to grasp?

Individuals

Are individuals:

- fit?
- in need of special consideration?
- trained?

	Example tasks	Short term action	Long term solution
	Loading and unloading deliveries by hand	Provide help for heavy loads. Reduce the load size.	Palletise loads. Use lift trucks, pallet trucks, boom conveyors, vehicles with tail lifts etc. 

Assessing and reducing risks

Example tasks	Short term action	Long term solution	
 Moving materials to and from machines	Break down the loads into easily handled units. Fold or wrap over large sheets of paper.	Use conveyors/ hoists/ lift trucks/ pallet trucks etc. Use air tables, eg at guillotines.	
 Loading and unloading machines	Raise pallets etc to the right height and position.	Automate load/unloading operations. Use mechanical aids, eg scissor lifts and pile hoists.	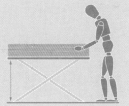
 Assembling and packing	Use appropriate, fit, trained personnel. Rotate the work to reduce repetition.	Provide a well lit working environment with suitable seating where appropriate. Automate. Provide mechanical aids.	
 Preparing, maintaining, moving and repairing presses and other equipment	Use appropriate, fit, trained personnel. Ensure adequate working space.	Provide mechanical aids, eg hoists for removing cylinders etc.	

Repetitive handling

Repetitive handling can present particular problems and give rise to conditions called work-related upper limb disorders (WRULDs) or upper limb disorders (ULDs). Sometimes the condition is called repetitive strain injury (RSI).

The musculoskeletal system (ie the muscles, bones, ligaments, tendons) in our hands, arms, shoulders and neck can be harmed by static or awkward postures, excessive force levels and repeated exertions. This is especially so when these are combined with little opportunity for variety or other means of recovery.

WRULDs can cause all of the following:

- pain;

- soft tissue swelling;

- restriction of joint movement;

- reduced sense of touch and manual dexterity;

- permanent disability if other symptoms go untreated.

Failure to take prompt action can result in the following:

- serious ill health. Well motivated and productive people have had to give up work because of pain and disablement from WRULDs; others have been so badly affected that simple household tasks become difficult;

- lost production due to employees taking sick leave;

- compensation claims from employees that have had to stop working because of WRULDs;

- employees complaining of, or seeking medical attention for, persistent pain or actual injury;

- hidden costs, eg training new staff or providing extra staff where sickness absence is high. Substantial cost savings can occur when a preventive strategy is adopted.

Additional information about ULDs is given in a free publication *Work-related upper limb disorders in the printing industry* (IACL91). See the References section for a list of priced publications.

To protect your employees from ULDs you need to be able to identify hazards which put them at risk and take steps to reduce the risk.

How to assess and tackle ULDs

Identify the hazards

The following are examples of operations which can give rise to ULDs:

- Use of powered hand tools.

- Use of pliers, scissors.

- Sealing boxes with tape.

- Hand feeding/unloading of machines.

- Assembly work.

- Counting, sorting, checking.

- Stripping, breaking, knocking-out, knocking-up.

- Flat pack wrapping.

- Hand handling of bundles.

- Hand insertion work.

- Jacketing of cased books.

Hazards may also exist if the work involves frequent, forceful or awkward gripping, squeezing, twisting, repetition, pulling, pushing or lifting.

Warning signs of ULDs can include complaints by workers and homemade, improvised changes to workstations or tools.

If any of the above are characteristic of your workplace you should proceed to a full ergonomic risk assessment. A systematic and ergonomic approach will assist in assessing risks and with providing solutions.

Reduce the risk

Apply ergonomic principles to machines, workstations and work methods so that the job fits the person. For example:

- reduce high force levels (maintain equipment properly, spread force levels, use tools with appropriately designed handles);

- reduce highly repetitive movements (balance frequent repetition with non-repetitive work, carry out tasks with the other hand, introduce handling aids, use automation, provide more varied tasks);

- provide rest/recovery time by breaks or activity changes before fatigue starts;

- change postures (modify operation, redesign work so the wrist can be straight);

- change the operator's position in relation to work;

- where people remain in the same position, provide a mix of work requiring movement.

Other steps include:

- making sure operators receive adequate information, instruction and training;

- being aware of the main causes/ symptoms and preventive measures;

- reporting problems early before they become serious;

- ensuring new employees start at slower work rate before gradual upgrading;

- rotating jobs (variation of tasks);

- ensuring that any incentive schemes do not adversely affect how the work is done (eg ensure sufficient breaks are taken).

Future control measures

Examine risks from ULDs when planning changes to work methods or purchasing new machinery. Check that ergonomic principles have been incorporated in the design.

- Consider health surveillance, eg record keeping and prompt medical assessment when problems are reported.

- Think about ways to encourage early reporting of symptoms.

- Look at sickness records and staff turnover.

- Consider the possibility of alternative work if a person cannot continue in a particular job or where it will assist a return to work.

- Introduce a system to monitor the effectiveness of current control measures.

- Be alert to any increase in ULDs in the workplace, for example after a change in process, and take appropriate action.

Radiation

Lasers

Laser use in the printing industry is increasing. Applications include laser printers and copiers, scanners,

platemakers, engravers (in printing cylinder manufacture), package date marking, die cutting and typesetting.

Radiation hazards

A laser is a source of intense light. Laser emissions can be dangerous when viewed either directly or when reflected from a smooth surface. The greatest hazard is to the eye, because it focuses visible laser emissions to form a very small image on the retina. Power intensities can be increased by a factor of 100 000 so that even a few milliwatts of laser emission can cause serious and permanent damage to the retina, and therefore vision in the affected eye.

It is important to get an eye examination immediately following hazardous personal exposure, but routine eye examination as part of health surveillance is not recommended. Some types of laser produce invisible beams that may still be focused by the eye to produce a harmful image on the retina. Skin burns may also be a risk that needs assessment.

Fume hazards

Laser copiers and computer printers may give off ozone, dust and fume, this is seldom excessive and not normally a problem if the equipment is both well maintained and sited in a well ventilated place. Other types of equipment may need local exhaust ventilation (LEV): your COSHH assessment will help you to decide the need for this, and your supplier should be able to advise.

Mechanical and electrical hazards

As with any machinery, dangers from moving parts and from electrical installations exist; these hazards should be evaluated as part of your risk assessment.

Safeguarding standards

Laser products are classified in accordance with their level of hazard. BS EN 60825-1:1994 gives information on class definitions. Laser products used in the printing industry will generally be Class 1 (safe by engineering design). This means the laser and workpiece will be fully enclosed during normal use.

Lasers are generally classified according to their output power, but remember that a Class 1 laser product may contain a high powered Class 4 laser inside its casing. Tampering with or removal of shielding or enclosure from a Class 1 product may result in exposure to a high-powered laser emission. Also remember that harmful exposure can result from reflected laser beams as well as those that are viewed directly. Avoid use of mirrors or reflective glass near laser sources.

When you acquire laser equipment the supplier has a duty to provide adequate information to you (see the section on 'Acquiring machinery and other work equipment' in Chapter 5). The information provided by the supplier will help you develop suitable systems-of-work for the safe operation of your equipment.

Only a competent person (usually a service engineer) should carry out any servicing or other work on your laser equipment. A competent person is someone who is properly trained in laser safety and who is able to follow a system-of-work which in many cases will include wearing suitable eye protection. It is your responsibility to assess eye protection needs and to ensure that your workers wear it - see the section on 'Personal protective equipment (PPE)' later in this chapter.

For further information on lasers see the booklet *Laser safety in printing*.

Ultraviolet (UV) light

UV light is used in photoengraving and lithographic platemaking and to cure certain inks, vanishes and lacquers, eg in lithographic, flexographic and label printing (see the section on 'Hazardous substances' earlier in this chapter for hazards of UV cured inks etc).

UV light is typically generated by carbon arc, xenon discharge tube or mercury

CASE HISTORY

An employee was dealing with a film misfeed on an imagesetter. He turned off the computer but forgot about the raster image processor (RIP). He opened the cover to the film and laser, and used an override key to run the film through manually so that he could find the misfeed. But stored information in the RIP caused the laser to start up unexpectedly, and the employee suffered eye damage from the reflected laser emission.

vapour discharge tube. Nowadays, carbon arcs are seldom used because of the fume they generate (primarily carbon monoxide and toxic oxides of nitrogen).

Radiation hazards

Excessive UV exposure can cause acute effects such as redness and burning of the skin and damage to the eyes (possibly causing painful conjunctivitis). The onset of symptoms may be delayed for several hours after exposure. UV exposure also increases the risk of developing various types of skin cancer and is associated with accelerated skin ageing and cataracts. Skin cancer risk increases with exposure level and with exposure time and is not thought to have an exposure threshold below which there is no risk.

When considering acute effects, as a general rule UVB sources, those emitting at wavelengths between 280 and 320 nm (nanometres), are more hazardous than UVA sources, those emitting at wavelengths between 320 and 400 nm. UVC sources emit below 280 nm and are potentially the most harmful. UVC radiation is, however, easy to remove as even glass is a heavy absorber. This is a technically complex area, and users may need to take advice from their suppliers about the adequacy of their precautions.

Fume hazards

UV light sources used for curing purposes are usually much more powerful than those used in platemaking. It is important to ensure that where these lamps are air-cooled they are well ventilated so that fume and any ozone is removed.

Safeguarding standards

Fixed or interlocked screening at UV light units prevents direct or reflected UV emission from being emitted to the workroom where it would present a risk to the skin and eyes. It is important that the screens, shutters and sealing brushes on print-down frames are well maintained, so that emission leakage is prevented. It is particularly important to check that lamp

Screen all UV light sources adequately, preferably with automatic curtains

cowlings are adjusted so that UV escape, especially where reflective substrates are in use, is minimised. A common failure is the splitting of infill canvas screens. These should be regularly inspected and replaced as necessary.

Printed sheets should not be visually inspected under a UV lamp because levels of reflected radiation may be high: remove sheets from the press before inspection.

For some unusual maintenance work it may be necessary to run a UV lamp without screening. In such cases, suitable eye protection against UV emission will be necessary, together with clothing to cover exposed areas of skin.

For further information see the booklet *Safety in the use of inks, varnishes and lacquers cured by ultraviolet light or electron beam techniques* and the sections on 'Screen printing' and 'Basic rules of machinery safety' in Chapter 5.

Infra-red sources

Infra-red units are used typically for drying printed material at offset litho presses, as an alternative to the use of anti-set-off powder and for accelerated drying. The equipment may be fitted retrospectively to existing machines.

Radiation hazards

Infra-red light may cause eye injury (especially to the lens of the eye). In the printing industry, however, it is unlikely that sources will be of sufficient output for this risk to be a serious problem. Exposure may also cause reddening and burns to the skin.

Fume hazards

The inks used on litho presses have a low solvent content and there are generally no fire, explosion or fume hazards arising from their evaporation. However, there may be some ink breakdown, particularly when printing on thin stock. You will need to assess fume hazards arising from your use of solvents and provide local exhaust ventilation (LEV) for high risk applications. Also bear in mind that it may be necessary to provide LEV for applications that produce offensive odours.

Safeguarding standards

Interlocking of lamp units with presses prevents the risk of fire when machines are stopped during a print run, or when there is a misfeed.

Dryers should be electrically isolated during wash-up at machines and use of flammable solvents avoided on the infra-red unit itself. Lamp enclosure may be necessary to shield operators from excessive exposure and to reduce levels of glare that might otherwise interfere with work.

Static eliminators

Static electricity may be a problem in some plants. As well as the possibility of operators experiencing painful static shocks, there is also the risk of static ignition of flammable vapours, for example where volatile, flammable solvents are used in processes such as web-fed gravure and flexographic printing. Polythene, PVC and other insulating substrates are particularly likely to generate static.

Static eliminators are used to prevent the build up of unwanted electrostatic charges and thereby avoid the potential for static ignition of flammable vapours. Static eliminators need to be of a design incapable of producing incendive sparks, and where relevant need to be constructed to a suitable explosion protection standard. Static eliminators may be used in conjunction with 'static assist' devices, or may be used to control static generated by the movement of the web.

Some static eliminators contain small amounts of sealed radioactive material, which ionises the air. It is also possible to use static eliminators such as carbon fibre brushes, and high voltage types, which do not contain radioactive material.

It is important that static eliminators are kept clean and properly maintained.

The correct fitting of any static eliminators is a skilled task and it is recommended that advice is taken from the suppliers. Static eliminators containing radioactive material should not be tampered with or dismantled. If you suspect they are not working correctly, call the supplier.

Health surveillance

Health surveillance is any activity that involves obtaining information about an employee's health and which assists in protecting that employee from health risks at work.

The main objective of health surveillance is to protect the health of individual employees by early detection of adverse changes which may be caused, for example, by exposure to noise or to a substance hazardous to health.

Health surveillance and the law

Health surveillance is one component of the overall management of health risks. It may be necessary:

- under COSHH, for example to protect against dermatitis or occupational asthma;

- under the Management of Health and Safety at Work Regulations 1992, where people work in noisy processes;

- or where there is significant exposure to lead in premises such as traditional craft printers and the Control of Lead at Work Regulations 1980 apply.

The need for health surveillance should be decided as part of the assessments required by these Regulations.

Health surveillance should not replace proper control measures but form part of a health conservation programme.

Health surveillance is required where:

- an identifiable disease or adverse effect may be related to exposure;

- there is a reasonable likelihood of the occurrence of that disease or effect occurring under the particular work conditions;

- there are valid techniques for detecting signs of the disease or adverse effect and surveillance is likely to improve the protection of employees' health.

All employees will need to be given information, instruction and training about any risks to their health that might arise from their work. Where health surveillance is appropriate they also need to know:

- what symptoms and signs to look out for, and where appropriate, how to self-examine (eg for dermatitis);

- how the health surveillance scheme operates and who to report to if they are concerned; and

- what the arrangements are for seeing their own health records and collective results of the health surveillance programme.

Records must be kept where health surveillance is carried out to comply with COSHH. The information that should be held in the records is detailed in the Appendix of the COSHH general ACOP (L5), see the References section for information on this.

Health surveillance in practice

Health surveillance will detect adverse ill-health effects, and can also help management to monitor the effectiveness of process controls.

The procedures below offer guidelines for health surveillance for both dermatitis and hearing loss. Health surveillance will also need to be considered when work involves exposure to lead or substances, such as isocyanates, that may cause occupational asthma. (See the booklet *Safe use of isocyanates in printing and laminating* for further guidance.)

Skin disease (dermatitis)

Where there is exposure to substances which may cause dermatitis and the hands and forearms are likely to be affected (for example where UV curable inks, lacquers and varnishes are used) the following measures will help to protect employees.

- Arrange for a responsible person such as a supervisor or first aider to be given training by an occupational health doctor or nurse on the symptoms and signs of dermatitis, and set up a system of periodic skin inspections. The frequency of the inspections will depend on the individual circumstances, eg the likely severity of the dermatitis that might develop, but would normally be at least every six months.

- Arrange for new employees to have their hands and forearms inspected before they start work with the substance that might cause a skin reaction.

- Refer any employee found to have relevant symptoms or signs to a suitable medical practitioner (normally an occupational health physician) who is familiar with the risks of the process and the principles of health surveillance.

- Train employees so that they can recognise and report relevant symptoms and signs of illness to the responsible person.

Hearing loss

Under the Management of Health and Safety at Work Regulations 1992, employees exposed to certain types of risk, such as high noise levels, should be provided with appropriate health surveillance. Such conditions are likely, for example, at large web-fed presses and associated folders. Health surveillance for hearing loss usually involves hearing checks called audiometry. The following measures will help employees.

- There is no simple formula to show when audiometry is necessary. The starting point is to assess the risk of employees becoming deaf because they are being exposed to loud noise. This risk depends on the noise level and the length of exposure. Employers should arrange for a competent person to carry out an assessment of their employees' noise exposures, as required by the Noise at Work Regulations 1989.

- It is good practice for employers to carry out regular hearing checks on all employees whose daily personal noise exposures equal or exceed 90 dB(A), ignoring the benefit that might be provided by hearing protection.

- However, the risk of hearing damage rises significantly at exposures above 90 dB(A), so employers should normally provide hearing checks when noise levels reach or exceed 95 dB(A), except where that exposure is likely to be temporary, say for only for a few weeks in a year.

- Programmes for hearing checks need to be under the control of someone who can make sense of audiometric data and advise individuals on the state of their hearing and on follow-up action. This might be an occupational physician, a nurse with appropriate training and experience, an audiological scientist or a trained audiometrician able to refer employees to a more qualified person when they need more advice.

Health surveillance for employees in noisy jobs normally means:

- regular hearing checks in controlled conditions to measure the sensitivity of hearing over a range of sound frequencies;

- informing them about the results of their hearing checks;

- keeping records; and

- encouraging them to seek further advice from a doctor where hearing damage is suspected.

For more information, see the leaflet *Ear protection in noisy firms - employer's duties explained* (INDG200) and guidance note *A guide to audiometric testing programmes* (MS26).

Occupational health services

Employers may need expert and specialist advice on how to help them with issues such as:

- identifying health hazards, assessing risks and choosing the necessary control measures;

- checking the effectiveness of the control measures and, where required, measuring the exposure of employees, for example by atmospheric sampling;

- advising on placement and rehabilitation of employees;

- provision of appropriate on-site first-aid and treatment facilities;

- identification of causes of ill health within the workforce;

- promotion of good general health among employees.

Occupational health services may be able to assist in these matters. HSE's Employment Medical Advisory Service can advise on services available in your area and the leaflet *Selecting a health and safety consultant* (INDG133) provides more information.

Other health issues

Workplace stress and mental health

Workplace pressure can keep staff motivated and be the key to a sense of job satisfaction, but people's ability to deal with pressure is not limitless. Excessive workplace pressure and resulting stress can be harmful and damaging to both your employees' health and to your business performance.

Where pressures are intense and continue for some time, the effects of workplace stress can lead to a number of physical and mental ill-health problems such as heart disease, high blood pressure, depression and anxiety. Employers have a responsibility under the HSWA to take reasonable care to ensure that health is not put at risk through sustained levels of stress arising from the way the work is organised, the way people deal with each other or from day to day demands.

It is known that too little personal control over the work, not being allowed to use skills fully, being overworked or underworked, and boring work can all contribute to stress.

Learn to recognise signs of stress and encourage employees to discuss problems openly - are people distracted, tense or worried?

Give help, be sympathetic and, if appropriate, advise employees to see their doctor. Delay can make matters much worse.

Further information on stress at work can be found in the employer's guide *Taking action on stress at work: a guide for employers* (HSG116).

New and expectant mothers at work

Employers are required to take particular account of risks to new and expectant mothers when carrying out risk assessments.

Particular attention should be given to lifting and carrying, hours of work including night work, work requiring long periods of standing and work involving exposure to chemicals, for example exposure to lead.

If a risk is identified then suitable alternative work should be offered. If this is not possible the worker should be given paid leave for as long as possible to protect her health and safety and that of her child.

Further information can be found in the booklet *New and expectant mothers at work: a guide for employers* (HSG122).

Drugs and alcohol

The misuse of alcohol and drugs can affect work performance and potentially pose a threat to health and safety. Employers can benefit by developing an alcohol and drugs policy. This policy should form part of the overall health and safety policy. It should help employers identify problems at an early stage, encourage affected people to come forward for help and treatment and ensure appropriate controls.

Some areas of work, such as operating machinery or driving, demand clear thinking and sound judgement. Employees whose performance is impaired by either alcohol or drugs should not be allowed to undertake these duties.

The Employment Medical Advisory Service of HSE can advise on all aspects of occupational ill health including drug abuse. Further information for employers is available in the leaflet *Drug abuse at work* (INDG91).

Passive smoking

Passive smoking is the breathing in of other people's tobacco smoke. It can cause damage to health, make asthma worse and cause lung cancer.

Think about agreeing rules with the workforce to protect non-smokers and encouraging and helping smokers to give up. Advice is given in the booklet *Passive smoking at work* (INDG63).

The Workplace (Health, Safety and Welfare) Regulations 1992 require that rest rooms and rest areas include suitable arrangements to protect non-smokers from discomfort caused by tobacco smoke. This can be achieved by providing separate rest areas or rooms for smokers and non-smokers or by prohibiting smoking in rest areas and rest rooms.

Humidifier fever

Humidifier fever is a flu-like illness caused by inhalation of fine droplets of water from humidifiers which have become contaminated by micro-organisms. It should not be confused with legionnaires' disease (see under 'Legionellosis').

The symptoms of humidifier fever vary from mild fever with headache, malaise and muscle weakness, to acute illness with high fever, cough, chest tightness and breathlessness on exertion. The onset of symptoms is delayed, beginning four to eight hours after the start of the working shift. The symptoms usually occur on the first day back at work after a weekend or other break and tend to resolve over 12 to 16 hours.

Humidifiers are sometimes used in print companies to stabilise paper size and condition. They are also present in building air conditioning systems.

Contamination of humidifier systems is most likely to occur in internal reservoirs within the humidifiers and in holding tanks, especially if the water is recirculated. Paper dust or anti-set-off powders may act as a nutrient for the growth of micro-organisms if allowed to accumulate. Exposure then results from spray emitted from the contaminated system.

So far, cases of humidifier fever in the printing industry have been associated with spinning disc and spray-type humidifiers incorporating holding reservoirs.

Prevention and control

Choose the humidification equipment that is least likely to become contaminated, eg steam humidifiers, compressed air atomisers that take water directly from the mains, evaporative type humidifiers that do not create water spray.

Maintain cleanliness: weekly cleaning may be necessary in process environments, every two to three months may be acceptable for offices.

If humidifier fever is suspected, turn off the humidifiers and seek advice from both a medical practitioner and a competent ventilation engineer with the necessary specialised knowledge of humidifiers.

Further information on avoiding humidifier fever can be found in the free leaflet *Humidifier fever in the printing industry* (IACL28).

Legionellosis

Legionnaires' disease is a pneumonia that principally affects those who are susceptible due to age, illness, immunosuppression, smoking etc and may be fatal. Legionellae can also cause less serious illnesses which are not fatal or permanently debilitating but which can affect all types of people.

Infection is attributed to inhaling legionellae. These bacteria are widespread in natural water sources but may multiply under certain conditions if they enter man-made systems or water services. Most cases and outbreaks of legionellosis have been attributed to water services in buildings and cooling towers; other sources may include humidification systems and industrial coolants. Plant and systems containing water which is likely to have a temperature in the range 20-45°C, and which may release a spray or aerosol during operation or when being maintained, may also present a risk.

Technical guidance on the prevention and control of legionellosis can be found in *The control of legionellosis including legionnaires' disease* (HSG70).

The law

The Notification of Cooling Towers and Evaporative Condensers Regulations 1992 require the notification to local authorities of wet cooling towers and evaporative condensers.

The prevention and control of legionellosis (including legionnaires' disease) Approved Code of Practice (L8) gives guidance on complying with the requirements of the Health and Safety at Work etc Act and the COSHH Regulations in respect of this risk.

Local exhaust ventilation (LEV)

Maintenance, examination and test and the law

Under regulation 9 of COSHH, control measures must be maintained in an efficient state, in efficient working order and in good repair. Regular maintenance will ensure this is achieved. Employers must also ensure that thorough examinations and tests of LEV are carried out every 14 months, and appropriate records must be kept for at least five years.

Maintenance, examination and testing of LEV has to be carried out by someone who has the necessary training, knowledge, skills and experience. Your insurance company may have the competence required.

Selection and use

LEV is frequently used and can be an effective way of controlling exposure to hazardous substances. It works by drawing hazardous emissions away from the breathing zones of workers into a hood or booth and ductwork connected to an extract fan. LEV may also be used on machines for controlling hazardous substances at the point at which they are generated.

Examples of situations where LEV might be necessary include:

- screen printing and screen cleaning work;

- gravure printing using volatile solvents;

- UV units where ozone or ink fly is generated;

- hot melt glue stations and paper milling at adhesive binders.

In many circumstances LEV may be cheaper and more effective than general ventilation. (General dilution ventilation works by introducing fresh air into the workplace to lower the general level of hazardous substances in the air.)

Heat losses from LEV may be minimised by heat recovery systems or recirculation of filtered air. Recirculation should only be employed after specialist advice to prevent the recirculation of hazardous materials in harmful quantities.

Making the most of LEV

Get an expert to design and install the most appropriate system, with the right hoods/enclosures, ductwork, air velocities and cleaning and filtration systems. It is sensible to involve employees in discussions about the design of the systems, as they have to use the plant and will have views about what is workable.

- Keep the extraction as close to the source of contamination as possible.

- Make sure the fan draws air away from the operator.

- Extract at the same level or below the source of contaminant unless there is need to control fume rising from a heated source. Extraction positioned above the

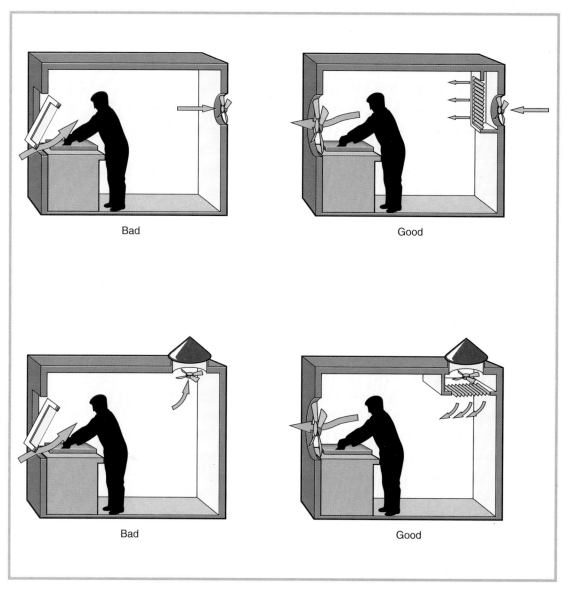

Make sure fans draw air away from the operator

operator's head will draw harmful substances into their breathing zone.

- Check and maintain the system regularly, particularly flexible ductwork.

- If necessary, provide sufficient heating and lighting (suitably protected) within the enclosure to encourage work to be done inside the extracted area.

Common causes of LEV failure

The following are common causes of LEV failure and are easily checked yourself. It helps to keep a record of these checks:

- physical damage to and poor positioning of hoods and booths;

- damaged and/or blocked ductwork;

- blocked, damaged, unsuitable or incorrectly installed filters;

- too high/low water levels in wet collectors;

- wear, corrosion or build-up of contaminant on fan blades;

- slipping or broken drive belts to fans;

- poor lubrication of fan bearings;

- poor fitment of the ductwork.

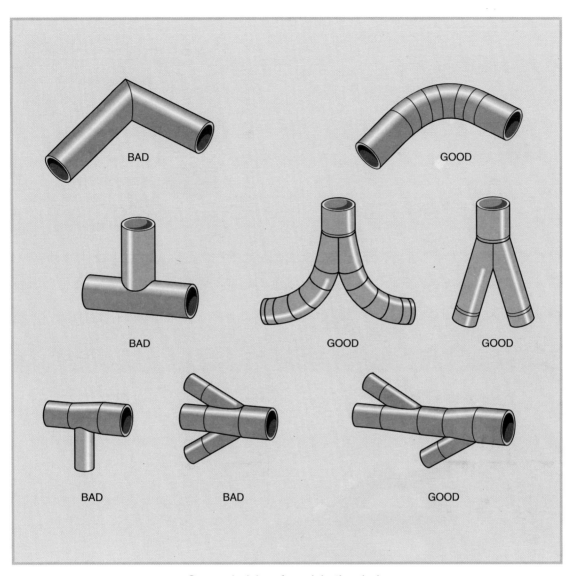

Some principles of good ducting design

Personal protective equipment (PPE)

If you are thinking of using personal protective equipment (PPE) to control employees' exposure to substances hazardous to health, remember that COSHH limits its use to situations where it is not reasonably practicable to use other control measures such as LEV.

PPE and the law

The Personal Protective Equipment at Work Regulations 1992 require employers to:

- assess risks to health and safety which have not been avoided before providing PPE;

- provide suitable PPE free of charge to protect employees against risks which have not been controlled by other means;

- take all reasonable steps to ensure it is properly used;

- maintain PPE provided in clean and efficient working order with appropriate storage accommodation for it when it is not in use;

- give information, instruction and training in its use.

Employees must use PPE provided and report any loss or obvious defect to the employer.

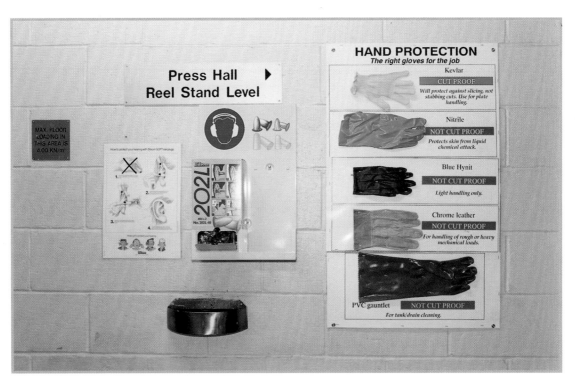

Employers need to provide suitable PPE and information

An example of respiratory protective equipment

Respiratory protective equipment (RPE)

Choosing

When choosing respiratory protection consider the job to be done in detail. Identify the contaminant and the likely level of exposure against which protection is required and take into account the working environment in which it will be worn.

Different types of RPE offer different levels of protection and the correct type has to be matched against the job, including the potential levels of exposure and the wearer. Assess the work carefully and consult the suppliers of the substance in use and protective equipment. British (BS) and European (EN) Standards set out the specifications for respiratory protective devices and filters. Check that equipment is marked to indicate conformity with a standard. Unless it is a good fit and properly worn, RPE will not offer effective protection and will not perform as designed.

Maintaining

Thoroughly examine and, where appropriate, test RPE at least once a month and more frequently where conditions are severe. (This does not apply to one-shift disposable respirators.) Half-mask respirators used only occasionally against dust or fumes of relatively low toxicity may be examined at longer intervals, but not less than once every three months. Make sure employees have facilities to clean respirators and know how to do this without damaging them.

Ensure that breathing air supplied to air-fed equipment is satisfactory; proprietary equipment to do this is widely available.

Storage of PPE

Suitable accommodation should be provided for PPE when it is not in use. The storage should be adequate to protect the PPE from contamination, loss, or damage by, for example, harmful substances, damp or sunlight. Where PPE becomes contaminated during use, the accommodation should be separate from any provided for ordinary clothing, and where necessary be suitably labelled. Special arrangements may have to be made to clean PPE. Make sure you inform your cleaners about any hazards.

Eye protection

Eye protection will have to be provided and used (sometimes throughout the whole workshop) where work which puts eyes at risk is carried out, eg:

- the use of pressure cleaning appliances which leads to the projection of spray and particles;

- the use of harmful substances, such as solvents which may splash into the eye;

- in maintenance departments, grinding and other machining processes, which lead to the uncontrolled ejection of metallic particles.

BS EN 166 sets out the standard for eye protection for industrial and non-industrial uses. Special arrangements are appropriate for people who normally wear glasses such as the use of goggles or safety glasses.

Hearing protection

See the section on 'Noise' earlier in this chapter.

Protectors should:

- be suitable for conditions in which they are to be used;

- provide sufficient attenuation to reduce the noise exposure level to below 90 dB(A) and preferably to below 85 dB(A);

- only be issued on a personal basis;

- never be removed in a noisy environment;

- be compatible with other forms of necessary PPE;

- preferably be marked to indicate conformity with a harmonised standard - BS EN 352.

Hearing protection and the law

In relation to ear protection, The Noise at Work Regulations 1989 require in outline:

- ear protection to be made available on request if the daily personal noise exposure exceeds 85 dB(A);

- that ear protection must be provided and worn if the daily noise exposure exceeds 90 dB(A).

Foot protection

Consider the provision and use of foot protection where there are risks of foot injuries, for example from heavy printing cylinders being moved. Anti-static protective footwear may be necessary in certain print works.

BS EN 345 and 346: 1993 set out the specification for safety footwear for professional use.

Chapter 5

PROCESS SAFETY

■ ■ ■ ■ ■ ■ ■ ■ ■ ■ ■ ■ ■

See the References section at the back of the book for details of publications which relate to PROCESS SAFETY and also see Appendix 1 Safeguarding terms

Relevant legislation

The Health and Safety at Work etc Act 1974 requires employers to ensure, so far as is reasonably practicable, the health safety and welfare at work of their employees. This duty extends to the provision and maintenance of plant and machinery that is safe and without risks to health.

The Provision and Use of Work Equipment Regulations 1992 place general duties on employers to ensure that the work equipment they provide is suitable and safe for use.

Manufacturers and suppliers have duties under the Supply of Machinery (Safety) Regulations 1992 (amended 1994) to provide new equipment that meets certain essential health and safety requirements and is safe. Employers, however, should still assess all equipment to ensure it is safe and free from patent defects before bringing it into use.

The Provision and Use of Work Equipment (PUWER) Regulations 1992

The main requirements of the Regulations (due to be amended at the end of 1998) which will need to be met by employers in the printing industry are to check that

● equipment is suitable for the use that will

be made of it and is not used for unsuitable applications (eg unprotected electrical equipment in flammable areas);

● equipment is adequately maintained (eg by carrying out the recommended six-monthly examinations of guillotines);

● adequate instruction and training is given to operators, eg platen press and guillotine operators;

● new equipment (including second-hand equipment from outside the European Economic Area) conforms with product safety legislation, eg Supply of Machinery (Safety) Regulations 1992 and amendments.

More specific duties cover:

● guarding of dangerous parts of machinery, eg in-running nips at cylinders and rollers;

● protection against specific hazards, eg disintegration and ejection of slitting discs;

● ensuring that control systems and devices are unambiguous, reliable and perform all the tasks necessary for safe operation, eg provision of emergency stop and other controls where appropriate;

● provision of adequate lighting, eg at test sheet removal area of a sheet-fed press;

Relevant legislation (continued)

- ensuring maintenance can be carried out safely, eg provision of ladderways and working platforms on large web presses for maintenance of free running rollers;

- ensuring that equipment can be isolated from sources of energy, eg electrical isolators or isolating gas valves at heat-set ovens;

- ensuring stability of equipment, eg bolting of racking to floor.

Basic rules of machinery safety

Every year serious accidents occur in the printing industry as a direct result of unguarded or inadequately maintained machinery. Just because you haven't had an accident at a particular machine, don't assume that the machine is safe. Machinery may need upgrading to meet today's safety standards. Do a risk assessment to check whether your guarding is suitable, then take any necessary action to reduce risks. (See the 'Planning and risk assessment' section in Chapter 1.)

The following are examples of basic steps you can take to reduce the risk of machinery accidents at work:

1 Choose the right machine for the job.

2 Check that it is adequately guarded, eg is there protection from in-running nip hazards at inking rollers and printing cylinders, is transmission machinery enclosed, are all interlocks working correctly, are gap covers provided and used?

3 Ensure operators and supervisors are adequately informed, instructed and trained so they know how to work safely and how to use the guards and safety devices provided. Some machines, including guillotines and platen printing machines, are extremely dangerous.

Young people in particular are likely to need additional training and a high level of supervision.

4 Check adequate lighting has been provided for work at all machines.

5 Provide clear working space around machinery.

6 Test and check machinery regularly to ensure safeguards are working.

7 Carry out maintenance work on a proactive rather than reactive basis.

Machinery guarding

In essence, all machinery must be guarded so that access is not possible to dangerous parts. Wherever possible, fixed guards should be used. However, if regular access is needed to dangerous parts, eg cylinders, then interlocking guards, trip nip bars, nip bars, electrosensitive safety systems or a combination of the above will be more appropriate. European Norm (EN) Standards give specifications for new machines. However, some of these standards may be relevant to existing machines.

Guards should be carefully designed, constructed and fitted to ensure that they are:

- in line with the safety reach distances laid out in BS EN 294: 1992 so that openings in or around guards do not allow access to the dangerous parts;

- sufficiently robust;

- not heavy or awkward to use (eg some gap covers and lift-off interlocked guards provided for flexo presses);

- designed to allow operators to see certain machine functions (eg gluing unit on a adhesive binder);

- designed to be compatible with machinery operation (eg fitting of wash-up trays);

- of adequate electrical/electronic integrity (eg suitable for use within flammable atmospheres at gravure presses), and sufficiently reliable for a safety application;

- are located sufficiently close to rollers if they are nip bars (ie no more than 6 mm from the cylinder surface);

- designed so that they do not cause a hazard themselves.

Identifying basic machinery hazards

The following are examples of machinery hazards, some or all of these may be relevant to your workplace:

Parts of the body, clothing and cleaning cloths can become entangled in rotating and in-running parts such as inking and damping rollers, printing cylinders, nipping rollers or transmission machinery.

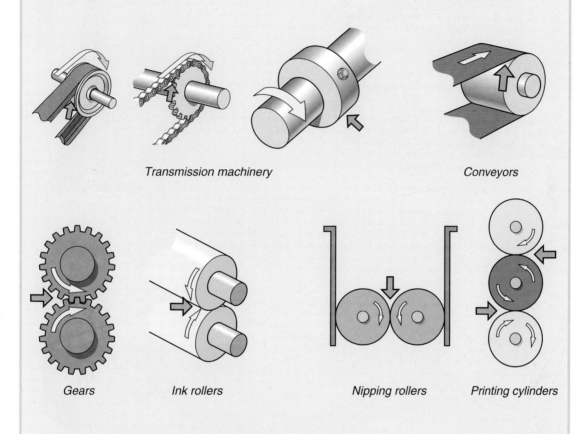

Transmission machinery   *Conveyors*

Gears   *Ink rollers*   *Nipping rollers*   *Printing cylinders*

Shearing can occur between parts moving past one another.

(a)   (b)

When a cylinder has a gap in it as shown in (a), a gap cover which completes the periphery of the cylinder as shown in (b) can be fitted. This eliminates the shear trap which arises when the cylinder rotates passed the fixtures.

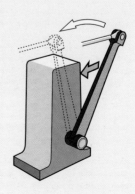

Crushing can occur between parts moving towards each other or between fixed and moving parts, eg the traps between gripper bars and machine body on certain litho presses, traps created by closing scissor lifts or traps created between moving parts of machines and fixed structures, eg litho proofing presses.

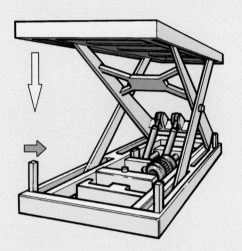 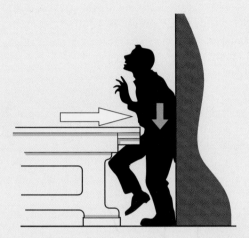

Cutting and severing can occur at sharp edges or surfaces, eg web-severers, slitters and guillotine blades.

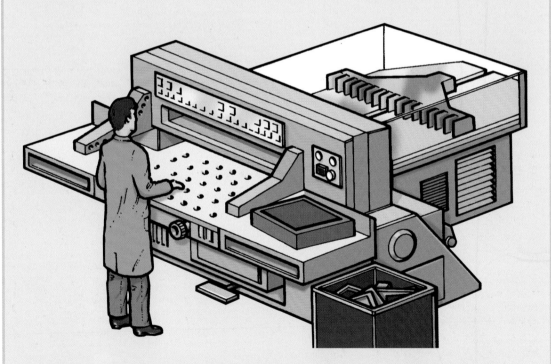

Materials can be ejected from machinery, eg reels from reelstands and hot glues from adhesive binding machines.

Electricity can also cause accidents at machines. Electrical hazards are covered in Chapter 6.

Interlocking guards

Opening an interlocked guard should stop movement of dangerous parts before they can be reached. Alternatively, guard locking can be used to prevent the opening of guards until dangerous movement has stopped (this is particularly appropriate for machines with long rundown times). Interlocked guards should be used where there is a need for frequent access, for example more than once a shift.

Machine controls

Control switches should be clearly marked to show what they do. Emergency stop controls should be provided where necessary, eg red mushroom-headed buttons within easy reach of operator positions that stop all dangerous motion and require positive resetting.

Operational controls should be designed and placed to avoid accidental operation, eg by the use of shrouds on start buttons and pedals. Presses with reverse facilities should have the reverse controls distinguishable by touch. This is usually done by the use of deep shrouds. Hinged flaps can also be used.

Multi-manned presses should have audible pre-start warning devices which automatically give an audible warning when an inch, crawl or run button is depressed. An acoustic signal of one to three second duration should be given. From the moment the signal is activated, at least three seconds should elapse (waiting time) before the machine can be started by repeated activation of the same or different control element.

After the waiting time or after a preceding operation in the inch mode (not continuous run mode) the machine can be started within 0 to 12 seconds (release time) without another audible warning.

After the release time or activation of the stop control, or the emergency stop, it should only be possible to operate the machine after repeating the whole of the above sequence. See the diagram on page 70.

Zoning of controls should be used on multi-manned presses or other equipment where the vision of a second operator may be obscured. A zoned control will only allow limited movement (slow crawl or inch) of a specific press area with a guard open, such

---

Integrity of guard interlocks

Guard interlocks can fail as a result of age or rough treatment. They should be designed to work in the positive mode so that under normal circumstances a failure of the interlock switch prevents machine operation (see diagram).

Switch A is installed in the positive mode, ie the contacts have been opened by the positive mechanical action of the cam. Switch B is installed in the negative mode, ie the contacts are opened by spring pressure when the cam is rotated. When switches are used singly, the positive mode should be used. Failure should prevent operation of the machine. Positive switches are also more difficult to defeat. The use of two cam-operated switches positioned next to each other but operating in opposite modes provides an even better standard.

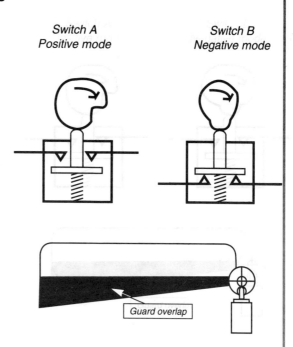

*Switch A
Positive mode*

*Switch B
Negative mode*

Guard overlap

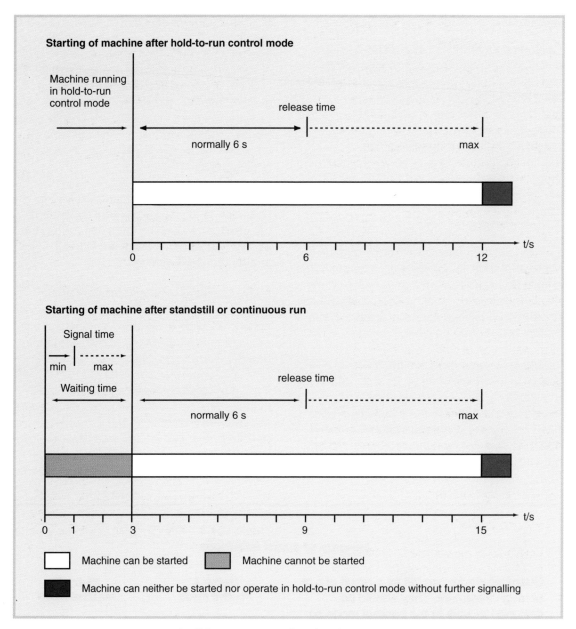

Starting of machine after hold-to-run control mode

Machine running in hold-to-run control mode

release time

normally 6 s

max

0   6   12   t/s

Starting of machine after standstill or continuous run

Signal time

min   max

Waiting time

release time

normally 6 s

max

0 1   3   9   15   t/s

☐ Machine can be started   ▨ Machine cannot be started

◼ Machine can neither be started nor operate in hold-to-run control mode without further signalling

Audible pre-start warning signal sequences

as one side of a print unit, or a single section of a gatherer-stitcher-trimmer, unless all other guards are in the correct positions.

Where dangerous parts have long rundown times, interlocking methods incorporating braking and/or guard locking should be used. Systems should be designed to incorporate a device to either cause the hazard to be eliminated as the guard is opened (by applying a brake), or prevent the guard from being opened until the risk of injury from the hazard has passed (guard locking). European Standard BS EN 1010 requires

guard locking to be provided on new presses with rundown times in excess of ten seconds.

Safe systems of work

A safe system of work is an agreed, documented, safe job method based on risk assessment that is designed to reduce the risk of accidents or ill health. Examples are the 'inch-stop-clean' or 'inch-stop-lock-clean' safe systems of work which minimise the risk of fingers being drawn into in-running nips.

ACCIDENT

An operator was cleaning the blanket cylinder of a press on continuous slow crawl. The rag he was using was drawn into the nip between the plate and blanket cylinder. The press was fitted with a trip-nip bar which stopped the machine but only after the printer's hand had been taken in up to the wrist. The accident could have been prevented by using the inch-stop-clean safe system of work.

Inch-stop-clean safe systems of work should be used when cleaning plate and blanket cylinders of litho presses. Cleaning should be carried out by a single operator. The cylinders should be inched and allowed to come to rest before cleaning. Hands should be removed before the press is re-inched.

Inch-stop-lock-clean or equivalent safe systems of work should be used when two operators are involved in cleaning one press. This system is also appropriate for cleaning impression cylinders. Locking involves the use of the stop lock button.

Other essentials

- Operators should know how to stop a machine before they start it.

- All guards should be in position and all protective devices working.

- Cylinder gap covers should be used where provided by the manufacturer.

- Hickeys (fluff) should only be removed from moving cylinders using a proper hickey picker (such as a rubber blade mounted on a wooden handle).

- Rags should never be applied to moving rollers or other parts such as duct rollers or oily transmission machinery.

- Lubrication or other maintenance work should be carried out with the power isolated.

Machinery maintenance

- All guards and other safety devices should be kept in good working order and checked regularly, eg daily and six-monthly checks on guillotines.

- Machinery should be isolated before maintenance work is carried out, especially if the work involves the removal of guards.

- Safeguards should be checked after any modifications to machinery.

- Maintenance needs should be considered prior to installing new machines.

- Preventive, rather than breakdown, maintenance procedures should be seriously considered.

Safety hazards by process

Origination

Design and art work

Although this is generally a low risk area, take care with scalpels which should be sheathed when not in use. Provide inclined lay-up boards with a high lip at the base to prevent scalpels falling from them. Dispose of used scalpel blades safely: don't just put them into wastebins.

Typesetting

Typesetting involves large amounts of work at visual display units (VDUs). The use of VDUs by the employed and self-employed is covered by the Health and Safety (Display Screen Equipment) Regulations 1992. Employers have a duty to make sure that the display screen equipment is safe and does not affect the user's health.

Workers using VDUs need well-designed work areas with suitable lighting and comfortable, adjustable seating. This helps to prevent undue tiredness, reduce eye strain, and prevent pains in the hands, arms, neck, shoulders and back. Place VDUs in a position where lighting will not cause reflections or glare on the screen. No special precautions are necessary against radiation;

the levels emitted from VDU equipment are well below the recommended safe levels.

Employers must:

- analyse workstations of employees covered by the Regulations and assess and reduce the risks;

- ensure workstations meet minimum requirements;

- plan so there are breaks or changes of activity;

- train and inform display screen users about the health and safety aspects of their work;

- provide eye examinations and tests for users on request and special spectacles where required - for a definition of users see *VDUs: An easy guide to the regulations* (HSG90).

Trailing electrical cables can cause accidents. Run cables in ducts, under the floor, around the walls or in a pendant dropped from the ceiling.

Computer equipment often generates large amounts of heat. Good general ventilation and/or air conditioning should cope with this. Automatic gas-flooding fire protection

systems may be used to protect major computer systems. Set up procedures to ensure that when personnel enter the protected space the automatic fire protection system is switched to manual and illuminated indicators provided to show the system's operating mode.

Platemaking

Screen all UV light sources adequately. Screening on printdown frames can take the form of curtains (preferably automatic or interlocked), automatic shutters or automatic roller blinds. Blinds should be maintained in good condition. Brushes should be used to reduce leakage of UV light around the periphery of the frame on printdown boxes.

On large format printdown frames, as found in screen printing, the UV sources should be positioned so that light is directed away from doors, windows and passageways, and screened from other work areas, eg by using curtains. Timer switches (or other on/off controls) should be located outside the screened area.

Rollers on automatic litho plate developers need periodic cleaning. The best method is to remove the rollers prior to cleaning. In-running nips need to be guarded (this is usually achieved by using interlocked

Graphic reproduction

Contact frame light sources should usually be screened. Where the contact frame has a low level UV source, screening with automatic curtains is desirable.

Rollers on automatic film developers will require periodic cleaning. The best method is to remove the rollers prior to

cleaning. In-running nips on automatic film developers should be guarded (this is usually achieved by using interlocked guards) except where the rollers are held in position by their own weight and the maximum force that could result is 50 Newtons. Rollers should not be cleaned while the machines are running as fingers may be drawn into in-running nips.

Provide laser containing equipment such as scanners and image setters with interlocked covers as part of the laser beam screening to ensure that Class 1 conditions are met (ie the output of the laser light is inherently safe) and to prevent access to rotating parts of machinery.

See the 'Radiation' section in Chapter 4 for more information.

guards) except where the rollers are held in position by their own weight and the maximum force that could result is 50 Newtons. Rollers should not be cleaned while the machines are running as fingers may be drawn into in-running nips.

Plate bending machines need to either be adequately safeguarded or provided with a simultaneous two-hand control. On plate punching devices the movement of the punching tool should be safeguarded either by design or by providing guards.

During flexographic platemaking moulding presses are frequently used to impose heat and/or pressure to rubber or synthetic compounds. The closing movement of these presses should be safeguarded. Local exhaust ventilation should be provided for the heat and fume generated. Also consider extraction for solvent wash-off from photopolymer plates and personal protective equipment such as suitable gloves where there is a possibility of skin contact with uncured photopolymers. (See the section on 'Personal protective equipment' in Chapter 4.)

Letterpress typesetting

Fit type- and line-casting machines with guards to protect against splashes from molten metal and remember hazards from lead dust and fume.

Guards and eye protection screens on metal saws should be in position and properly adjusted. Small pieces of metal should only be cut on saws with sliding feed tables and clamps to reduce the risk of injuries.

Proofing

The danger of hands being trapped in the shear traps created by the moving carriage of litho proofing presses should be eliminated. Trip devices should be provided at each end of the carriage which actuate a fail safe stop device to arrest movement of the carriage.

Where hazardous in-running nips exist at the stationary damping and inking roller units, they should be guarded, eg by fixed nip bars. Many litho proofing presses avoid this hazard by having 'lift out' rollers or stopping these rollers when the carriage moves away.

The inking and damping rollers on the moveable carriage should be safeguarded either by interlocking guards, fixed nip bars or other effective means. The action of 'sheeting off' is a hazardous operation which should be prohibited.

Regularly maintain and check safety features on all proofing presses.

Office/in-plant type equipment

Many offices now have photocopying equipment, while in-plant print departments may have a complete range of smaller size equipment. The safety precautions needed are virtually identical to those laid out in the other paragraphs of this section though some very small equipment may have insufficient power to harm anyone.

Take precautions to ensure that strong light sources in photocopiers are adequately shrouded and that access to dangerous moving parts and high voltage equipment is prevented. Carry out handling and changing of toner, and provide adequate ventilation to prevent build up of heat and ozone, in accordance with the manufacturer's instructions.

Hand-operated guillotines need to have an adequate blade guard fitted.

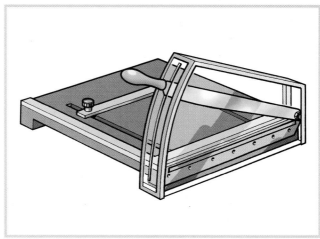

Hand-operated guillotines require blade guards

Printing

Litho sheet-fed

Where access to moving parts is needed, eg for some cleaning or make-ready operations on printing machines, the guard control circuits should be interlocked so that with guards open the machine can be operated by hold-to-run controls only. The hold-to-run control devices should be designed to allow:

- machine movement limited to 25 mm (true inch) on each depression of the control or a maximum operating speed of 1 m/min; or

- where the measures defined above would reduce the ability of the machine to perform its function and where there would be no substantial increase in risk,

machine movement limited to a maximum of 75 mm (limited inch) or a maximum operating speed of 5 m/min.

Where interlocked guards allow hold-to-run, slow crawl or inching, cylinder nip bars should be provided to minimise the risk of entanglement in contra-rotating rollers or cylinders.

Nip bars can be provided in the form of fixed nip bars (which should be located within 6 mm of the cylinder surfaces for pre-1997 machines or 4 mm for new machines), or 'trip nip bars' which stop printing cylinder movement within the deflection travel distance of the bar. Trip nip bars should be provided in preference to fixed nip bars on newer presses. Maintain all nip bars so they function correctly.

Emergency stop controls should be provided within reach of all operating positions

Two colour press fitted with slotted, interlocked, all-enclosing guards

On multi-manned presses an audible pre-start warning device should be fitted

Reverse hold-to-run controls should be touch-distinguishable, eg by use of shrouds, flaps etc to prevent inadvertent operation.

Access is often required to inking and damping rollers, especially to apply wash-up solvent. Interlocked rod type or slotted all-enclosing guards interlocked to the machine drive should generally be fitted so that powered movement cannot occur with guards in the open position. Where the manufacturer has designed nip bar type inking roller guards, these are acceptable as long as they are maintained in position.

Inking roller guards should be compatible with the wash-up tray and any adjustments should be possible from a safe position. Any auxiliary damper roller drive motors should be interlocked with the appropriate damper roller guard so all movement is stopped with the guard open, or additional nip bars should be provided.

There are various safeguarding arrangements that can be used to reduce the risk of injury by the plate, blanket and impression cylinders. The hierarchy of control measures is outlined below. The standards outlined at the top of the list should be used where possible, those at the bottom of the list may be acceptable for older presses:

- interlocked all-enclosing guards plus trip nip bars;

- interlocked all-enclosing guards plus fixed nip bars;

- trip nip bars plus gap covers (plus good stopping performance);

- fixed nip bars plus gap covers (acceptable on certain older machines only).

Note: fixed nip bars should be set at no more than 6 mm from the cylinder surfaces, you may need to adjust the gap to meet this requirement on older presses.

Guarding is required for the dangerous parts of feed tables, including:

- in-running nips associated with chains and sprockets;

- rotating shafts;

- swing arm grippers;

- trolley wheels.

Transfer cylinders and delivery mechanisms need high standards of guarding due to the severity of injury they cause. Interlocked and/or fixed guards are essential. The interlock arrangement should only allow the press to be 'inched' due to the severity of the hazard and usual lack of nip bars. The delivery mechanism guarding should permit the safe removal of test sheets.

Clearly mark all press controls. Emergency stop controls should normally be provided at all operating consoles and within easy reach of all other operating positions and print stations, and should stop all hazardous movement. On certain smaller existing presses without powered inching/crawling, additional emergency stop controls will not be necessary as they will not enhance the overall safety of the machine. Control stations on units should preferably be laid out so that hold-to-run controls are above, or immediately adjacent to, the emergency stop controls.

On multi-manned presses, or those on which it is not possible to clearly see all over the press from any control station, an audible pre-start warning device should be fitted (see under 'Machine controls' in the 'Basic rules of machinery safety' section earlier in this chapter).

Safe methods of work are essential for the safe operation of presses. The inch-stop-clean system should be used when cleaning plate and blanket cylinders. In this method the cylinders should be allowed to come to a complete halt before cleaning. Hands should be withdrawn from the danger area while 'inching' the press.

Cleaning the impression and transfer cylinders can be awkward and hazardous because they are often inaccessible, have no nip bars, and have an extra hazard created by the grippers. The inch-stop-lock-clean method should be used when cleaning this area.

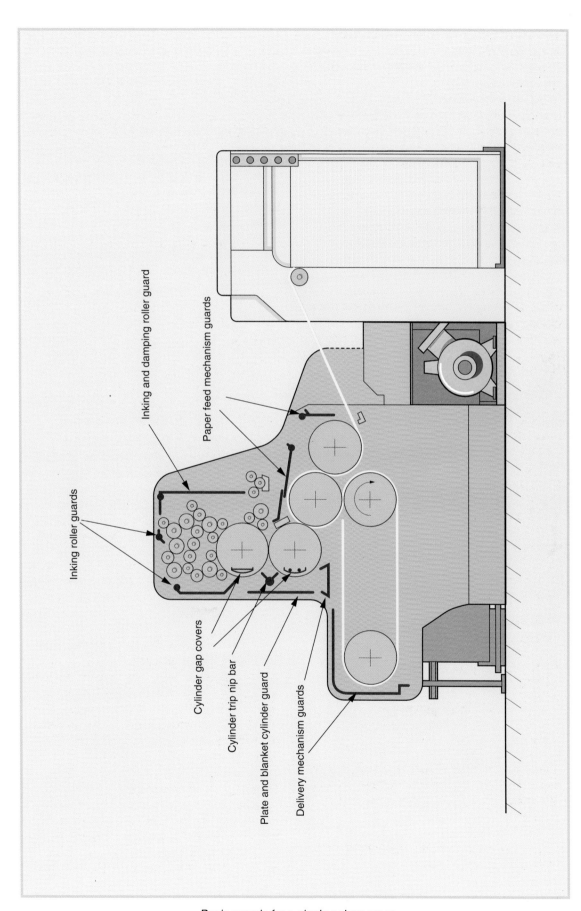

Inking and damping roller guard

Paper feed mechanism guards

Inking roller guards

Cylinder gap covers

Cylinder trip nip bar

Plate and blanket cylinder guard

Delivery mechanism guards

Basic guards for a single colour press

The inch-stop-lock-clean method should always be used when two or more operators are cleaning any press cylinders unless the press has guard zoning.

Presses should not be manually cleaned on continuous slow crawl because the risk of serious injury due to the in-running nipping hazards.

Guards and other protective devices need to be regularly maintained and checked. A weekly audit of the guards, their operation, the hold-to-run controls and the emergency stop control should ensure that presses remain properly guarded.

Hickeys (fluff) should never be removed from a moving cylinder except with a proper

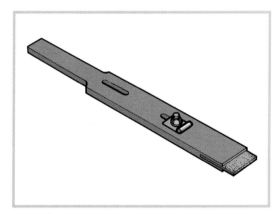

Hickeys should not be removed from moving cylinders except with a proper hickey picking stick

hickey picker. Rags should never be applied to moving inking or damping rollers including duct rollers, even if adjacent rollers are well guarded, because of the risk of entanglement.

Reel unwinds and rewinds

For the purpose of this book, the terms reel unwinding and rewinding devices apply to simple single reel, non-automatic equipment for the provision and collection of paper webs. The term reelstands applies to larger installations capable of holding two or more reels and installations associated with automatic operations such as splicing.

The following safeguards are appropriate for reel unwind and rewinding devices:

- Unwind units are usually of two types, shafted or shaftless. On unwinds the in-running nips between the reel and pressure roller should be protected either by a trip device or guards.

- In-running nips associated with the pressure/rider rollers should be guarded over the entire reel diameter. This may be achieved by the provision of trip devices or area interlocked guards. Devices for bringing the reels up to speed should be guarded if danger points are accessible, for example at running tension belts.

- Any shear hazards created by movement

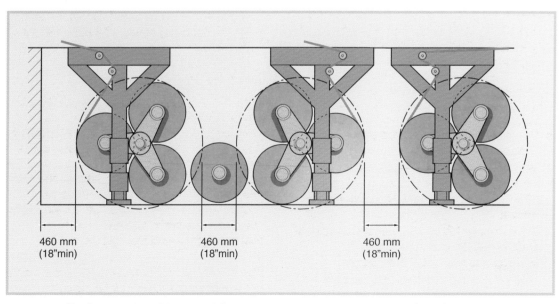

460 mm (18"min)   460 mm (18"min)   460 mm (18"min)

Reelstands should have a minimum 460 mm clearance between reels or fixed parts of the reel lifting arms or other reel lifting devices should either be guarded or reel lifting/lowering should only be possible using hold-to-run controls restricted to a speed of no more than 5 m/min.

- Where shaftless unwinding or rewinding is used, the chucking cones should be designed so they can only be inserted using a hold-to-run control. The hold-to-run speed should not exceed 5 m/min for new machines. The control system of the machine should prevent start up until the chucking cones have been fully inserted.

- Ejection of a reel due to a 'core chew out' or inadvertent opening of the chucking cones must be prevented. The controls should not allow separation of the chucking cones while the press is in motion.

Safeguards for reelstands

- Existing reelstands should have a minimum 460 mm clearance between the surface of the largest reel that the stand is designed to accept and any obstruction such as a full reel mounted on an adjacent stand or wall unless fixed or interlocked barriers prevent whole body access.

- Since any reel being loaded will encroach on the 460 mm gap mentioned above, reels should not be left standing within the reelstands on the sub-trucks.

- Perimeter fence guarding should also be provided where hand/arm access is possible to in-running traps/nips created between rotating and stationary reels on the same reelstand unless a minimum separation distance of 120 mm can be maintained between the reels.

- Additional dangers created by an adjacent stand indexing during automatic splicing will need to be addressed, for example unexpected start up of the reel, splicing unit movement and spider arm movement. A safe system of work should be implemented to address such hazards in conjunction with safeguarding. Safeguarding may be provided by electrosensitive devices and trip bars.

- Where turrets or spider arms rotate

automatically, pressure-sensitive mats or similar should be provided to prevent rotation when a person is in the pit. Where rotation is manually controlled, movement should be by means of a hold-to-run control.

- Where reels are driven by belts on the reel circumference, the danger point between the reel and the belt should be safeguarded by interlocked or other effective guards. Guards should also be provided to protect operators from in-running nips created at drive belt guide rollers.

- Where flying splicing devices are fitted, they must either be safeguarded by fixed and interlocked guards or be 'safe by position' (ie out of reach of any work platform).

- On presses fitted with reelshafts, guards or loose sleeves need to be provided for any exposed ends of the shafts. Any brake discs should also be guarded.

- Safeguarding for draw and festoon/dancer rollers is necessary to protect operators from in-running nips and roller movement. This may be achieved by a combination of fixed nip bars, interlocking guards, tunnel type guards or by ensuring a spacing of at least 120 mm between the rollers.

- Ejection of a reel from a reelstand due to a core chew-out or inadvertent opening of the chucking cones must be prevented. The controls should not allow separation of the chucking cones while the press is in motion.

Web offset

Webbing-up presses following a web break and/or a format change is a hazardous operation. It is extremely important to ensure that a safe system of work is devised and a written procedure laid down and adopted. On new presses this will be supplied by the manufacturer. On older presses a safe system of work may need to be developed in conjunction with press crews, safety representatives and management.

The safe system of work should take account of the different web path configurations including paths through colour satellite units

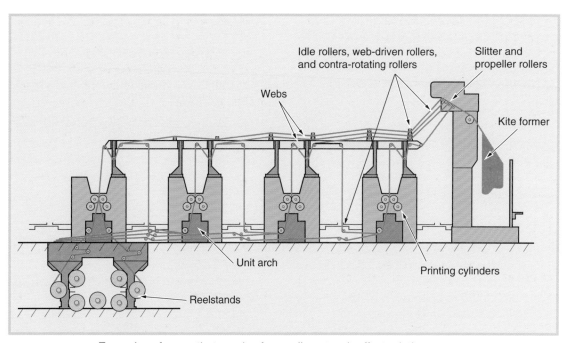

Examples of areas that need safeguarding at web offset printing presses

Newspaper printing

and through the folder, involving cross association if appropriate. It should also deal with the use of part-width webs where web lead-in devices may not be usable. The written procedures will need to include a clear diagram of the press showing all possible web paths.

Manual webbing-up should be carried out with the press stationary and off impression so that the web can be passed between/around the cylinders. Web lead-in devices can significantly reduce the hazard associated with webbing-up and should take the web from the reelstands, through the print units and dryers to the top of the folder, but not including turned or bay window web paths where the tapes may be terminated.

On older presses, or machines not fitted with web lead-in devices, the practice of tucking in or attaching the web to the cylinder with adhesive tape should be used so that all operators can withdraw completely and stand away from the press when the hold-to-run controls are depressed.

Traps associated with driven web lead-in tapes or chains should be guarded where there is a risk of injury, eg by providing disc guards.

Inking and damping rollers must be guarded (see under 'Litho sheet-fed' earlier in this section). On certain old installations the inking and damping rollers may be guarded by non-interlocked enclosing guards. These should be upgraded by providing nip bars or by interlocking the enclosing guards.

Plate, blanket and impression cylinders must be guarded. Guarding can take the form of robust fixed nip bars if the printing and blanket cylinder gutters are less than 4 mm deep and 8 mm wide (or exceptionally 19 mm wide on newspaper presses) and the presses throw-off (cylinder movement going on and off impression) still keeps the nip bars within 6 mm of the cylinders during make-ready and wash-up.

Ideally, nip bars should be supplemented by the use of all-enclosing interlocked guards which also guard the inking and damping rollers. Following web breaks, nip bars should be checked by operators to ensure they have not been deflected away from the

cylinders leaving gaps in excess of 6 mm.

Certain types of presses require some nip bars to be removed for make-ready. A hinged nip bar secured when the press is in the run mode is acceptable as long as measures are taken to ensure it is always in position when the press is run, eg by interlocking.

On unit arch type presses, access must be prevented to roller/cylinder intakes within the arch. This guarding can take the form of internal guarding, eg nip bars or fixed guards or interlocked unit gates. With interlocked gates open movement of rollers/cylinders within the arch should be via local hold-to-run controls only allowing crawl speeds of no more than 5 m/min (10 m/min may be acceptable in exceptional circumstances, eg on some older presses).

Web severers within unit arches and elsewhere on the press need to be guarded or be safe by design. Tunnel guards are frequently used. Precautions need to be taken to ensure that the web severers do not automatically fire when operators or others are in the vicinity, interlocked access gates to units can be used.

Due to the high speeds of many of these machines and the inertia of web-driven guide rollers, these rollers should be safeguarded. Guarding such as nip bars can be provided or the rollers can be separated from other contra-rotating rollers and the machines frame by a gap of at least 120 mm.

Ovens at heat-set offset presses may have opening hinged tops. Ensure that these will not close inadvertently, trapping the operators. The controls to close the oven should be of the hold-to-run type and be located so that the closing movement of the oven can be seen along its entire length.

A gap of at least 120 mm should be allowed between accessible in-running chill rollers, or a guard fitted. Guards should be fitted over the balance weights at the ends of the rollers if they are accessible.

Propeller and slitter roller intakes should be guarded. This guarding is often associated with dust collection hoods and should also

Propeller and slitter rollers should be guarded

eliminate the laceration hazard posed by slitters. The guarding should cover at least 300° of the roller.

To facilitate make-ready, cleaning operations etc, hold-to-run controls should be provided which may allow movement of the press with the interlocked guards open. On existing installations hold-to-run slow crawl speeds should be less than 10 m/min. Certain older installations may not be able to achieve this speed and the slow crawl speed at these should be as low as practicable.

On new installations hold-to-run controls should meet the hold-to-run standard set out under 'Litho sheet-fed' earlier in this section and zoned where the vision of additional operators is impaired by the press structure.

Clutches used to disengage the drive to press units should be provided with interlocks which ensure that the controls on a disengaged unit remain ineffective with the exception of the emergency stops.

Misinterpretation of indication lights on presses has resulted in a number of accidents. It is therefore extremely important that the indicator lights are clear and unambiguous.

Guard locking devices should be used where presses have a long rundown period. On new presses guard locking should be provided where the rundown period is in excess of ten seconds.

Guard all in-running nips and other mechanical hazards on folders. In-running nips should be protected with nip bars and/or enclosing guards, eg nipping and cross association rollers. Guidance on folders is given under 'Label printing' later in this section.

Consider incorporating noise control measures in enclosing guards and, where possible, controls, locking nuts and adjusting devices should be brought outside danger areas, by extending them through the guard.

Flexographic

Safeguarding of unwind and rewinding units is explained under 'Reel unwinds and rewinds' earlier in this section.

Safe webbing-up procedures need to be implemented. Much of the advice under 'Web offset' earlier in this section is applicable though many older presses will not have web lead-in devices.

Flexographic printing units on all size presses, eg label presses to flexible packaging presses, are a frequent source of accidents. It is particularly important to ensure that they are properly guarded.

Removable enclosing interlocked guards or gate/barrier interlocked guards are generally considered acceptable. The former are usually more suitable for small- to medium-sized presses, and presses with web widths up to 1 m, and the latter for larger machines.

Adjustable nip bars have not proved satisfactory as they are frequently removed or incorrectly adjusted (due to the use of stereo cylinders of variable diameter). They are only likely to provide a satisfactory standard of protection on presses which carry out long-run work with few or no cylinder changes where strict controls are in place to ensure they are always correctly adjusted.

gravure/impression intake and impression/back impression (boule) rollers. These should be designed so that they can be adjusted to within a maximum of 6 mm from the surface of the cylinders and are often best mounted off the doctor blade carrier. Safe systems of work will need to be implemented to ensure the nip bars are always used correctly.

Where presses are used for short to medium runs, guarding should be provided in the form of interlocking guards. These can either be fitted along the side of the presses or over individual print units. Give careful consideration to using flameproof interlock switches (see the 'Explosion risks in flexo and gravure' section in Chapter 7) and to the need for doctor blade wiping. Slots can be cut in the guards which allow the doctor blade to be wiped with a long pencil but prevent finger access to the dangerous parts.

As these presses are usually multi-manned, audible pre-start warning devices must be fitted (see Appendix 1). Use hold-to-run controls for make-ready, cleaning etc and develop safe systems of work for make-ready, cleaning and webbing-up etc (see headings 'Litho sheet-fed' and 'Web offset' earlier in this section).

Screen printing

Hinged or clam-type screen process printing machines with power closure should be fitted with efficient trip guards around the three edges of the screen unless the closing force is less than 300 Newtons and there are no sharp edges. These will stop the screen or make it retract if anyone becomes trapped. Regular testing of the safety devices should be carried out to ensure they continue to operate effectively.

On semi-automatic flat bed machines take precautions to minimise the likelihood of the reciprocating table striking the operator, by providing sensitive edges, presence-sensing devices or chain rails to prevent access. The traps between the vertically reciprocating frame-holder and the four main machine pillars will also need to be guarded.

On automatic cylinder screen printing machines all squeegee, cylinder and frame drives need to be adequately guarded. The 'gap' in the cylinder creates a shear hazard across the main frame when it is in motion. This is frequently

fitted with a gap cover which should be kept in position. The frame and screen also prevent access to this area so undersized frames should not be used unless the remaining areas of the frame-holder are infilled.

All drive gears/chains for the conveyors should be adequately guarded as should the trap between the conveyor belt and end drum/roller.

For more information see 'Screen printing and cleaning' in the 'Hazardous substances' section in Chapter 4.

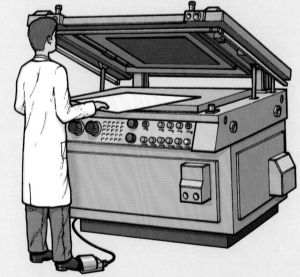

Hinged or clam-type screen printing presses with power closure should be fitted with safety trip bars

Lettterpress sheet-fed

Platen printing machines should only be operated by properly trained people. Hand-fed platens should be provided with an efficient trip guard, irrespective of whether they are power or treadle operated. These guards should be tested on a daily basis (see under 'Cutting and creasing' later in this section).

Automatic sheet-fed platens have not normally been provided with guards (other than the stirrup guard) for the reciprocating platen or the inking rollers. So it is particularly important that operators are properly trained and properly supervised.

Guards interlocked with the machine drive should be provided for the reciprocating forme of flat-bed presses. The most appropriate types of safeguarding are mechanical interlocking, or electrical interlocking with guard locking to take account of rundown times.

Inking rollers should also have an interlocked guard, preferably made of parallel metal bars to allow the application of cleaning solvent. Delivery mechanisms with travelling grippers should be effectively guarded as they can cause serious accidents. Impression cylinder guards should also be provided.

Maintenance work should never be undertaken on these presses without first electrically isolating the press, as the moving bed can be very dangerous.

Label printing machines

Presses with twin side frames should meet the standards laid out under the headings 'Web offset' and/or 'Flexographic' earlier in this section. Label presses of the cantilever type should meet the standards laid out below.

The gear wheels and in-running nips on cylinders and rollers of the print units on cantilever label printing machines should be safeguarded, for example:

- hinged or rise and fall interlocked guards; or

- removable enclosing interlocked guards.

Hinged or rise and fall interlocked guards are often designed to cover all print units with one guard. This often prevents operators from being able to make adjustments or add ink on the 'run' so provision should be made for these adjustments by extending controls/ink troughs through the guard.

Removable enclosing interlocked guards can be used to safeguard each print unit individually and, if properly designed, allow adjustments and topping up of ink while the press is running. Detailed information on their design is given under 'Flexographic' earlier in this section.

Some older machines may be provided solely with adjustable nip bars as guarding. These may only be accepted if they are always in position and procedures are set out to ensure their use. They are usually found to be removed or incorrectly adjusted, in such cases upgrading to interlocked guarding is appropriate.

Pacing/draw rollers should be provided with enclosing interlocked guards or suitable nip bars where access is possible to in-running nips created by contra-rotating rollers.

In addition to the enclosing guard on flexographic print units, a fixed nip bar should be provided at any in-running intake between anilox and duct roller as these rollers often have an auxiliary drive to prevent the ink from drying when the press is stopped. The distance between this nip bar and the surface of the cylinder should be no more than 6 mm. Low powered drives may also be acceptable if they prevent injury. On some presses a chamber doctor blade arrangement may be fitted. Adequate procedures should be laid down for the safe handling of doctor blades.

The dangerous parts of the finishing section of label printing machines must be safeguarded. These sections will comprise some or all the following units: rotary die-cutting units, flat bed die-cutting units, slitting knives, trim removal/rewind, punching units, perforating (cross and inline) etc. Combinations of fixed nip bars and interlocking guards need to be used to guard

these finishing/processing stations.
It is important to ensure that the guarding arrangements are adequate for all web paths including the different trim/label trim stripping paths. These areas often produce a lot of dust and high noise levels so the guarding arrangements should take these hazards into account.

To facilitate make-ready etc, label printing machines may be fitted with hold-to-run controls to allow operation of the press at slow crawl speeds with guards opened (see under 'Litho sheet-fed' earlier in this section).

In-line folders, sheeters, die-cutters etc

All in-running nips and other mechanical hazards on folders and other in-line processing equipment need to be guarded. Guard design may need to take account of other hazards such as noise and dust.

On new and recently installed folder installations, the folder should be totally enclosed with fixed and interlocked guards. Guard locking devices should be fitted where there is a high risk of severe injury (ie chopper folder) and the press has a rundown period of more than ten seconds even after actuation of the emergency stop control.

Totally enclosed folders should be provided with arrangements for the remote control of folder settings either by electrical/electronic or direct mechanical means. The bending rollers and delivery area are likely to be outside the 'enclosed area'.

The bending rollers need to be provided with a 'nose' guard at the base of the former (kite) and adjustable guards for the portion of the bending rollers behind the former. The delivery area must be adequately guarded. However, a hold-to-run guard override control button may be provided for the delivery tunnel guard. Depression of this hold-to-run control will allow operators to open the guard at speeds up to 8 m/min to allow removal of the first incomplete product copies.

All-enclosing guards may not be practicable on older folders and localised guarding of the dangerous parts should be provided. In these circumstances the following areas

need to be safeguarded: the nipping/pinching rollers, cross association rollers, folding drum, cutting cylinders, cross perforating cylinders, jaw cylinder, quarter folder etc. Dangerous nips between delivery belts and pulleys should also be guarded.

On sheeting units the main areas of danger are the draw rollers and the rotary knife. The draw rollers should be guarded by either fixed nip bars or enclosing interlocked guards. The rotary knife is a high-risk area and on a large installation should be guarded by a high-risk interlocking arrangement (ie dual circuit interlocking) and with the provision of guard locking if the rundown time is long enough to make it necessary.

Business forms presses

The dangerous parts of finishing sections of business forms presses must be safeguarded. These sections and the means used to guard them are the same as those for label printing machines. If wander leads are provided, allowing access to parts with guards open, they should be of a simultaneous two-hand control type. These may allow speeds in excess of 10 m/min where specified by the manufacturer and where there is appropriate guard zoning.

Where, on business forms presses, the web is delivered by a spiral folder as in a zig-zag folded continuous stationery pack, the delivery guard may be fitted with an enable guard override control button. This operates as a hold-to-run control allowing the guard to be opened at slow run speeds to facilitate removal of the first incomplete copies.

A minimum gap of 25 mm should be maintained between the spirals by the provision of adjustment stops. Where the spirals need to be closed to less than 25 mm, a local guard preventing access into the nip must be provided. Fixed guards must be provided for the spiral drive gears.

Conveyors, counters, stackers, tyers and strappers in publishing rooms need to be safeguarded

Publishing rooms

Types of conveyors, counters, stackers, tyers and strappers vary considerably so the guidance given below is general.

Effective means for stopping newspaper conveyors which enter the publishing room should be provided for use in emergencies. Where dump gates are provided at folders to divert copies, it should be possible to stop the insert conveyor leading to the publishing room without stopping the press.

Where dump gates cannot be fitted, it may be necessary to provide stop buttons in the publishing room which stop the press as well as the conveyors where these are mechanically linked. Normal press stops should be carried out from the press room, and a signalling system provided so that publishing room staff can request that the press is slowed down or stopped.

Overhead conveying mechanisms out of reach, ie 'safe by position' will not normally require additional guarding.

However, access may be possible to these mechanisms while they are running so some localised guarding may be required. Operators have been known to use ladders or movable steps for copy or blockage removal etc.

Counter stackers should be provided with guards preventing access to dangerous parts, for example rotating collection hoppers. Safety reach distances to prevent dangerous parts being accessed (see BS EN 294:1992, listed under 'Important machinery standards' in the References) will apply. Where guards have to be opened by operators, they should be interlocked to the counter stacker drive. Otherwise they should be fixed in position and require a tool for removal.

Conveyor-fed automatic string-tyers and strappers may be divided into two groups:

- those with a low-pressure clamp not capable of inflicting injury, eg less than 300 Newtons and where an elastic bottom plate cover has been provided;

- those with high-pressure clamps.

Machines which fall into the second category should be provided with a combination of fixed and interlocked guards preventing access from the sides, in-feed and delivery ends. Safety reach distances in BS EN 294:1992 apply. Lift-off guards and guards that need to be opened frequently for cleaning jams, replacing string etc will need to be interlocked, this will include any lift-up conveyor sections.

Some strapping machines may have force-limiting devices, eg slip clutches on the clamp as well as a resilient rubber facing for the clamp, and may have no other associated dangerous parts. Gravity-fall crucifix-turn devices can become dangerous when laden and screenguarding should be fitted. This may require interlocking if access to other dangerous parts is possible. Where you rely on force-limiting devices, these should be regularly tested using a load-cell pressure gauge or other suitable instrument.

Dangerous parts associated with conveyors such as belt and chain drives must be safeguarded including those situated below the conveyors. Lift-up conveyors on these units should be arranged so that access to dangerous parts is not possible when the conveyor section is raised, this is usually achieved by interlocking the conveyor section.

Where conveyors enter the publishing room from below, adequate barriers and toeboards should be erected around the conveyor and floor opening.

Control stations should not be located in the path of machine-mounted robot movements. Robots and personnel should be separated as far as possible. Trip wire/pressure-sensitive edge etc combinations need to provide adequate protection to operators. The integrity of the interfacing of these guarding devices with the programmable control systems of the robot should be assessed. Robots should be able to stop safely, without trapping operators or ejecting their load.

Copy pick-up points should be designed to prevent access to dangerous parts by providing fixed or interlocked guards.

Front and end covers of inserting and stitching drums should be interlocked so that when they are open only movement by hold-to-run slow crawl is possible. Adequate safeguarding should be provided at the rear of the drums to prevent injury when removing misfed copies.

Interlocked or fixed guards should be provided to prevent access to dangerous parts from working platforms or other areas. Overhead chain drives should be safe by position or guarded, full length guarding may be more practical than multiple localised guards. Stitching heads should be fitted with interlocked hood guards where otherwise accessible, eg from work platforms.

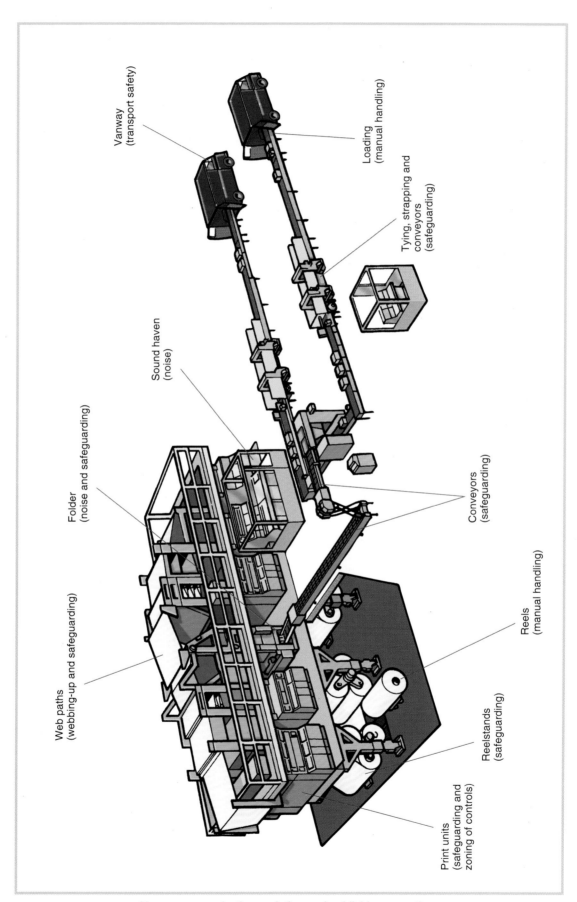

Vanway
(transport safety)

Loading
(manual handling)

Tying, strapping and
conveyors
(safeguarding)

Sound haven
(noise)

Folder
(noise and safeguarding)

Conveyors
(safeguarding)

Web paths
(webbing-up and safeguarding)

Reels
(manual handling)

Reelstands
(safeguarding)

Print units
(safeguarding and
zoning of controls)

Newspaper production - printing and publishing operations

Envelope-making machines

There are two broad categories of envelope-making machine, blank-fed or web-fed. Both types of machine usually consist of printing units, gumming station, window-patching station, folding and gluing station, a collator drum and a take-off section. Blank-fed machines have a feed plate or feed pillar. Web-fed machines will have a reelstand, profile cutting system and rotary or flying knife as well.

The dangerous parts of these machines include the in-running roller nips, gumming wheels, knives, reciprocating feed devices, gear wheels and drum-related shear traps; these must be safeguarded. Many of these dangerous parts can be guarded by fitting side guards to the machines. These should be interlocked to the machine's movement so that opening of any one of these guards stops the machine. Localised interlocked or fixed guarding can also be used. In-running nips on folding rollers where safeguarded by tunnel type guards may, in exceptional circumstances, have openings of 30 mm where the safety distance to the danger point is 200 mm.

Machines may be fitted with two-hand, hold-to-run controls for set up. The speed should be limited to 10 m/min and guard zoning provided. In exceptional circumstances, where the use of stroboscopes is needed at production speeds for fault-finding, the following should be provided:

- hold-to-run control;

- guard zoning;

- a selector switch;

- a safe system of work which includes use of the slowest speed possible.

Additional local fixed, interlocked and adjustable guards are necessary on many of the machines' individual units. The feed plate or feed pillar will need local profiled guards for the draw, hook rollers and any score rollers. Any hinged gumming units should be interlocked to prevent them being left out of position, exposing dangerous parts when not in use.

Standards for reelstands on web-fed machines should meet those outlined under 'Web offset' earlier in this section. The print units on both types of machine should be guarded in accordance with the standards set out under 'Flexographic' earlier in this section.

Seal flap, window and bottom flap gumming units will all require guarding to prevent access to in-running nips or contact with hot glues. All enclosing interlocked guarding may not be feasible as access may be needed to the glue bottles. A combination of fixed and interlocked guards is often most successful. Think about the handling of the glue bottles as this may pose a significant manual handling risk.

The intakes associated with the glassine tissue knife and tissue applicator in-running nips need to be guarded. Any shear trap between the delivery table and drying drum should be safeguarded. This may be achieved by providing fixed or interlocked guarding or a hinged table end of at least 25 mm. Any belt or pulley intakes should also be guarded. Delivery guarding can usually be achieved either by fixed tunnel guarding or by adjustable plates.

On web-fed machines areas of high risk include the profile cutting system and separating knife. These areas must be adequately guarded by providing fixed or interlocked guards. Guarding should take account of the rundown times of the knives and the frequency of access.

Noise can cause serious problems on envelope machines so it is often a good idea to combine guarding and noise reduction measures. New machines with high noise levels should be supplied with noise control measures incorporated as standard.

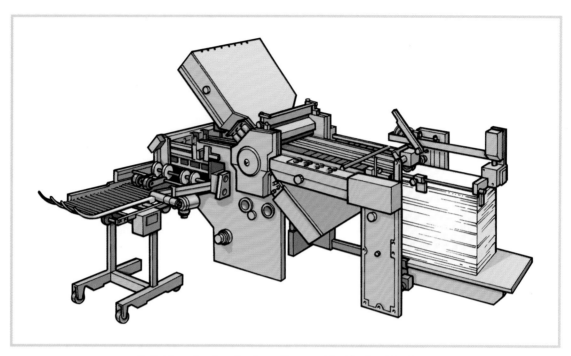

Suitable noise-hoods should be provided for buckle plates

Finishing and sheet-fed folding machines

The danger points on sheet-fed folding machines must be guarded. The two main types of machine, buckle and combination, give rise to similar risks. One of these is noise which can be addressed by providing suitable noise-hoods for the buckle plates. On new machines noise reduction measures should be provided as part of their standard specification. (See the section on 'Noise' in Chapter 4.)

The main in-feed rollers should be provided with fixed or interlocked guards with a narrow slot for sheet entry. Access to the folding rollers should be prevented by a combination of guards, the machine's frame and the buckle plates.

In-running nips associated with drive tapes should be guarded. This can be achieved by designing the transport/feed tables to 'fit' the pulleys, ie reach to a point no more than 6 mm from the in-running belt/pulley nip, or the provision of nip bars. Give particular attention to the nips associated with tensioning pulleys.

The dangerous parts involved with folding knives should be guarded. On new machines

this may be in conjunction with the delivery area of the buckle-folding unit, ie an all-enclosing interlocked guard. On older machines a more localised fixed or interlocked guard should be provided.

Perforators, creasing units and slitters are often fitted to this type of machine. The intakes associated with these devices should be guarded, including any in-running nip created between them and fixed parts of the folding machine. Precautions also need to be taken to prevent access to the periphery of running slitters and perforators.

When interlocked guards are in the open position the machine may be started for setting up operations using a two-hand hold-to-run control. The setting speed should be as low as possible and no more than 70 m/min measured at the folding roller.

Guillotines

Power-operated paper-cutting guillotines are potentially the most dangerous machines in the printing industry. They must be adequately safeguarded, regularly checked by both operators and competent guillotine engineers, and operators must be properly trained.

An unacceptable guillotine and work area

Guillotine fitted with photoelectric curtain and simultaneous two-hand-controls

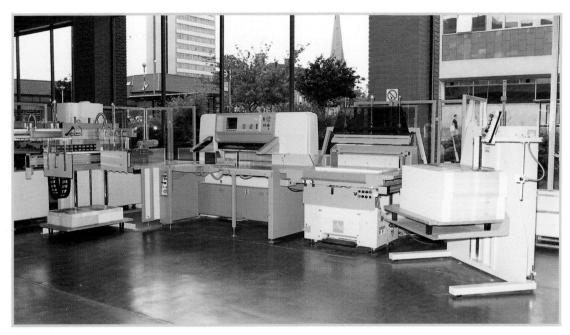

Modern guillotine and handling system

Further guidance on the guarding, maintenance and testing of guillotines is available in the booklet *Safety at power-operated paper-cutting guillotines*. This publication also contains information on training and knife change procedures.

COMMON ACCIDENTS

Amputations following double stroking of the knife due to faulty brakes and poor maintenance (including top dead centre cams).

Crush and amputation injuries by the clamp particularly when the dynamic gauging force exceeds 500 Newtons.

Amputation injuries caused by trapping fingers in the screw adjustment holes of clamp when the clamp returns.

Trapping accidents between the moving backgauge and clamp.

Accidents due to incorrect guard positioning or guards being defeated.

Accidents during knife changing.

Photoelectric (electrosensitive) safety systems

Photoelectric safety systems for guillotines should meet certain minimum standards with full function monitoring (FFM) as the lowest acceptable level for old machines. New machines will need to meet more stringent standards.

In general, guillotines supplied prior to 1974 with original photoelectric curtains will not be of the required safety integrity and new guarding systems will be necessary.

Guillotines supplied between approximately 1974 and 1987 should have electrosensitive safety systems designed and operating to full function monitoring (FFM) standards. However, on some guillotines certain modifications will need to be carried out such as the removal of the fully automatic facility. A competent guillotine engineer should be able to advise you.

Guillotines supplied after 1987 should accord with BS EN 61496 Part 2 (see 'Important machinery standards' in the References section).

Guillotines supplied after 1 January 1995 should be 'CE' marked and comply with the Supply of Machinery (Safety) Regulations 1992 as amended.

It is extremely important that the photoelectric curtain (light curtain) is located correctly. Serious injuries have occurred when the curtain has been incorrectly mounted and operators have accidentally reached over or under the curtain without breaking the beams.

As a general rule, the outermost beam should be located approximately 635 mm from the cutting stick and no more than 185 mm above the table.

Where new machines have a usable pile height of more than 185 mm, the outermost beam may be located at a position 610 mm minimum and 700 mm maximum from the cutting stick and no more than 205 mm above the table. An electrosensitive protective device (additional beam) should also be provided at a distance of between 400 and 550 mm from the cutting stick and at a height of between 0 and 205 mm above the table. An additional beam should be fitted on all new machines fitted with fully automatic cutting operation. Where the machine design is such that the curtain extends down to the machine table, the outermost beam should be at least 400 mm from the cutting stick if the beam is less than 38 mm from the table.

The separation distance of the curtain from the cutting stick must be consistent with the overall stopping performance of the machine. Older machines will generally have a distance of at least 460 mm between cutting stick and curtain.

Six key points to check on photoelectric safety systems:

● The system is of adequate integrity (see the book *Safety at power-operated paper-cutting guillotines*.

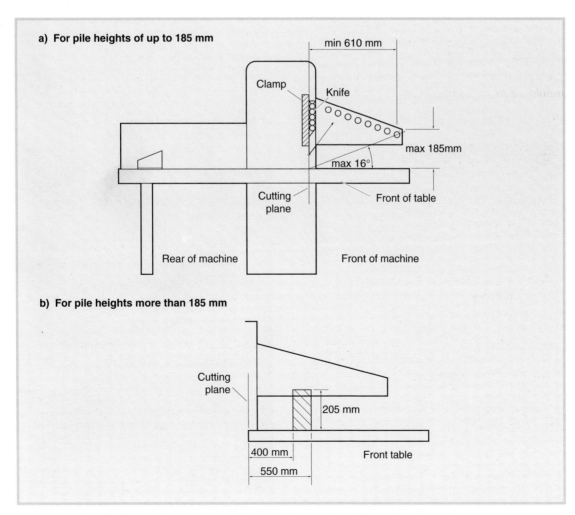

Positioning of the electrosensitive protective devices (beams) and curtain housing

- The photoelectric curtain is located correctly.

- Two final switching devices are provided for fully automatic machines.

- Simultaneous two-hand-controls are fitted.

- The dynamic gauging force of the clamp is less than 500 Newtons.

- Suitable rear table guarding is fitted (see 'Interlocking guards' below).

Body push guards

Body push guards fitted to guillotines are no longer considered adequate safety devices. Guillotines fitted with body push guards should have been withdrawn from service.

Interlocking guards

Four key points to check on interlocking guards:

- The guard prevents access to the danger zone (ie you shouldn't be able to reach over, around or beneath the guard when it is in the down position and lifting of the guard stops the machine before you can reach the blade or clamp).

- The interlocking arrangement is of the required integrity (this will normally need to be a dual channel control system - your supplier should be able to confirm this).

- Simultaneous two-hand-controls are fitted.

- Suitable rear table guarding is provided which prevents access to dangers created by the moving clamp, blade or backgauge.

Common requirements for all power-operated paper-cutting guillotines

Modifications to guillotine safety systems should only be carried out by competent guillotine engineers, manufacturers or suppliers because of the complexity of the systems and the potential dangers resulting

Automatic sweepaway guards

These are designed to push operators' hands away from the cutting area before they can be injured by the knife or clamp.

Five key points to check for guillotines fitted with sweepaway guards:

- The guard sweeps to a point 500 mm from the face of the clamp prior to the clamp or knife descending 50 mm.

- Addition guard bars/mesh have been provided to prevent access over/through the guard.

- Side access to the danger zone at the front of the machine has been prevented when the guard is extended, eg by providing large sidetables or fixed guards.

- Simultaneous two-hand-controls have been provided.

- Suitable rear table guarding is provided.

Sweepaway guards should not be changed for electrosensitive systems if a non-fail-safe brake is fitted.

An unacceptable sweepaway guillotine

from inadequate modifications.

Simultaneous two-hand controls should be fitted to all machines. Older machines may need their controls upgrading. The two-hand control should meet the following basic standards:

- both buttons should be operated within approximately 0.5 seconds of each other before the machine will operate;

- if one control is released, both buttons should have to be released and re-operated for re-initiation;

- the controls should not be capable of being spanned by one hand;

- if one or both controls are released, the machine should stop or return to top dead centre.

The above guidelines are very general and the detailed requirements of individual machine types and models should be checked with the manufacturer/supplier and against the guidelines in the book *Safety at power-operated paper-cutting guillotines.*

Operators should carry out daily tests and checks of guillotines fitted with electrosensitive (photoelectric) safety systems or interlocking guards. These checks should also be carried out after knife changing.

Sweepaway guards on guillotines should be checked by operators on a monthly basis. All tests should be recorded. The checks should also be carried out after knife changing.

Six-monthly examinations and tests should be carried out on all machines by competent and trained engineers and cover safety components (eg brake and clutches, interlock switches and cams), stopping performance and gauging pressures.

Further information and example test proformas can be found in the book *Safety at power-operated paper-cutting guillotines.*

The integrity of guards and braking systems on guillotines can only be maintained by regular testing and examination - failure to maintain a guillotine could result in a serious and avoidable incident.

Knife changing

Special precautions are necessary to prevent injury when knives are changed. The guillotine manufacturer's instructions should be followed. These usually entail procedures involving devices such as knife handles or slides and supports for safe removal, mounting boards for safe transport and storage, and the use of an assistant when changing knives on larger machines. Precautions should also be taken to keep others away during knife changing, eg by the use of barriers and a table near the front of the guillotine.

Cutting

Three-knife trimmers must be adequately guarded. This is usually achieved by providing fixed or interlocked guards. Provide interlocked tunnel type guards to prevent access to the knives from the rear of the machine.

Feedside guarding on manually fed machines should incorporate trip devices at the feed area, for example a tripped flap running the length of the feed opening or tripped side guards or both. The trip devices should operate at minimal deflection and should instantly cut power and movement of dangerous parts if an operator's hands are carried into the feed opening.

Provide adjustable feedside guards where book sizes vary. These will need to be maintained in the correct position to allow feeding of the work but prevent operator access to the danger area. Front table dimensions may need extending to give operators additional protection by distancing them further from the feed opening.

Emergency stop devices, including lift-up bar devices at certain older machines, are not a substitute for the trip devices referred to in the previous paragraphs.

Photoelectric curtains can also be used to provide protection at the feedside.

Simultaneous two-hand hold-to-run controls should be provided on new manually fed machines. Similar standards should be provided on older existing equipment.

You will need safe systems of work for knife changing, these systems should incorporate the use of knife covers.

Loose knife cutting machines must be adequately guarded. Manually operated single stroke machines are safeguarded through a combination of a sliding front feed table, simultaneous two-hand-controls and either localised fixed guarding for the sides and rear or perimeter-type fencing.

Automatic machines need a higher standard of safeguarding as the two-hand-controls only offer protection for the operator during the initial strike on. The feedside should be safeguarded by either a hinged interlock guard which has a reach distance/product feed opening complying with BS EN 294 or an electrosensitive safety system.

Locate the photoelectric curtain incorporated in this system correctly to prevent people reaching the danger points or being able to stand between the photoelectric curtain and machine. The sides and rear can be safeguarded by a combination of fixed and interlocked guards.

Shear and trapping points on the paper feed and take-off systems should be either designed out or safeguarded using trip devices or other methods.

Binding

The closing traps associated with the spine-forming devices and platens on hydraulic bookpresses should be guarded. This is best achieved by enclosing interlocked guarding.

The dangerous parts associated with the opening/closing and indexing of book clamps on adhesive binding machines should be guarded. This can often be achieved by all-enclosing interlocked guarding, though additional localised fixed and trip devices may be necessary at hand-feeding stations.

The milling cutter needs to be well guarded, typically by an interlocked all-enclosing guard and a self-adjusting/adjustable local guard. You can deal with cutter rundown time by using braked motors or guard locking. Minimise risks from hot melt adhesives by providing suitable screens or covers and adequate methods for refilling the adhesive.

On most types of case-making and case-in machines the dangerous parts can be adequately guarded by providing all-enclosing guards interlocked to the machine's drive. The feed and discharge parts of the machines should be outside the guarded area.

Blocking machines

The trap between the closing platens (one of which is often heated) on blocking machines is very dangerous and must be guarded. On automatic machines this can be achieved by the provision of all-enclosing interlocked guards.

On hand-fed upstroking or downstroking machines, the rear and sides of the platens can be guarded by fixed/interlocked guards. The front feed table should be provided with an adjustable (often rod type) pivoting guard, which trips if the bottom of the guard is pushed in, or a trip device and simultaneous two-hand hold-to-run controls.

Gatherer-stitcher-trimmers

Serious accidents have resulted at gatherer-stitcher-trimmers (GSTs), collator-stitcher-trimmers and gang-stitcher-trimmers, particularly through contact with the trimmer knives and through the incorrect operation of wander lead controls.

Fixed and interlocked guards should be provided for dangerous parts of the gatherer/feed stations. Interlocked guards normally take the form of hinged perspex lift-up guards, either for individual feed stations, or as a single guard covering all the feed stations. Interlocking is normally achieved through the use of positively operating cam switches. Users need to carry out regular guard checks to ensure safety is maintained. Under no circumstances should interlock switches be removed or defeated.

Problems can occur where single cam switches are provided for single guards covering all feed stations if the cam moves out of alignment, allowing operation of the

Fixed and interlocked guards should be provided for all dangerous parts of GSTs

stations with the guard raised. In such circumstances, upgrading to provide a second cam switch operating in the opposite mode, mounted by the side of the original switch, would achieve a higher standard of safety and should be considered.

Access should not be possible through or around guards to dangerous parts. BS EN 294 safety standards should be applied.

Fixed and/or interlocked guards should be provided for dangerous parts associated with the stitcher section including the stitching heads and calliper roll. Guarding may take the form of a single hinged perspex guard

fitted with a single cam operated interlock switch. Any interlock switch should operate in the positive mode. Access should not be possible through or around guards to dangerous parts.

The trimmer section usually consists of three guillotine blades or knives (the head and tail knives and the forage knife). The knives reciprocate automatically throughout the run. Guarding for the blades and other dangerous parts is essential. Guarding may take the form of a sliding tunnel guard or a large hood, split into two sections hinged at the middle. Access to the blades with the guards open will be required for knife changing and adjustment.

The guards should be interlocked by means of positively acting interlock switches. The switches will normally be cam operated. Care must be taken to ensure that the cams do not move out of adjustment; upgrading as outlined above may be appropriate. Regular guard checking is recommended. Opening of the guards while the blades are in motion must stop dangerous movement before a hand can reach a danger point.

Fixed guarding is usually not a suitable alternative to interlocked guards because of the need for frequent access.

Openings in the guards, including feed and delivery openings, should not allow access to dangerous parts. Where access is found to be possible through the delivery or other openings, guarding should be upgraded to prevent access.

Local two-hand hold-to-run controls or a two-hand hold-to-run wander lead can be provided which allow operation of the GST with one guard open. Single button controls are not acceptable. Two-hand-controls should meet the following conditions:

- They should require simultaneous operation in line with BS EN 60204 and be suitably positioned to prevent spanning by one hand. Controls that fail to meet this standard should be upgraded.

- With the gather/feeder station or the stitcher guard open (but not the trimmer guard) the machine may, in exceptional circumstances, run at speeds of more than 10 m/min although the speed should be set as low as possible.

- Setting, maintenance and knife change operations with the trimmer guards open should be a one person operation carried out by a trained operator who should be in control of any inch or pendant controls. Accidents have occurred when two operators have been working together and one has operated the wander lead while the other has had their hands in the trimmer section. The two-hand-controls or wander lead should not permit running or jogging of the trimmer section with the guards open. Operating the two-hand-

control with the trimmer guards open should allow no more than a single stroke by the trimmer blades however long the controls are actuated, ie if the controls are operated and held in for several seconds the trimmer blade should do no more than one stroke and then come to a complete rest.

Where operation of the knives is not restricted to a single cut with the trimmer guards open, machines should be designed to allow necessary running adjustments with guards closed.

Transmission machinery should be securely fenced. Standards for fixed or interlocked guarding should take account of the frequency of access. Machines should be designed so access is not required to dangerous transmission machinery on a frequent basis.

Precautions should be taken to prevent risks from lifting hinged guards falling under gravity.

Handwork

Guards are required on edge-gumming machines with nipping rollers and on the in-feed belts of edge stripping machines. Some machines used in metal comb (spiro) binding work can be dangerous; guards on the powered bar or platen of the machines which close the comb must be properly adjusted and kept in position. See the 'Office/in-plant type equipment' section earlier in this chapter for hand-operated paper-cutting guillotines standards.

Cutting and creasing - platen presses

Hand-fed platens used for cutting and creasing can be very dangerous. The main dangers are hand injury due to late feeding or taking out when the machine is in continuous operation, and body trapping due to accidental or inadvertent operation of the platen while making ready or clearing waste. These machines are split into two sizes, small machines with a platen width of up to 1 m and large machines with a platen width of greater than 1 m.

On small machines a trip guard should be fitted which closely surrounds the platen on three sides. A rise and fall guard may be provided on the front edge of the platen to ensure the minimum gap is maintained between the moving platen and the trip guard. A trip guard or pressure-sensitive edge should also be provided on the front edge of the moving platen.

On older mechanical brake/clutched machines a disconnecting device must be provided which ensures that if pressure is maintained on the operating foot pedal the trip guards will still function.

On large machines and all new machines capable of continuous run or timer-controlled operations, additional side guarding is necessary. This can take the form of pressure-sensitive mats or fixed side tables. The integrity of the control system and guarding circuits should be to a high risk standard, eg dual circuit cross monitored.

Where timer-controlled operation or a 'dwell' device is fitted, the 'dwell' period must not exceed 12 seconds.

The trip guards on both small and large hand-fed platens need to be regularly tested. Both of the tests outlined below should be carried out frequently enough to ensure that proper performance is maintained.

Test 2 should be carried out at least daily and be made when the machine is cold **and** when it is warmed up. The operator should carry out the tests but only following proper and careful instruction.

Testing should also be done periodically by a member of management or an engineer. All tests should be recorded and all records held. A suitable test piece would consist of a 12 mm cardboard tube.

Test 1

The actual tripping point should be tested by turning the machine over by hand. (This may not be feasible on larger machines.) When the trip device actually trips there must be a gap of no less than 175 mm or half way on machines with a travel of less than 350 mm.

Test 2

The stopping effect of the trip device should be tested with the machine running. The platen should come to rest no less than 90 mm from the frame, or on small machines where the tripping distance may be less than 175 mm, no less than 65 mm.

Letterpress sheet-fed presses are often converted to cutting and creasing machines. Safety standards for these converted machines should follow the guidance given under 'Letterpress sheet-fed' in the 'Printing' section earlier in this chapter. Inking rollers should be removed on converted machines, eg cylinder presses.

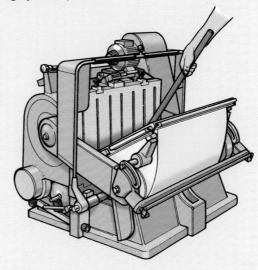

Testing a hand-fed platen

Other equipment

Stitching

Power-operated stitching machines should have a guard for the stitching head to prevent access when the work is in place. Guards provided for flat stitching on some machines are not effective during saddle stitching so a different profiled guard needs to be used, reversible guards are often supplied by the manufacturer. Operators should be trained to use guards correctly.

Book sewing

Automatic/semi-automatic machines should be provided with a combination of fixed and interlocked guards to prevent access to dangerous parts. Fit hand-fed machines with adequate trip guards to guard the sewing heads. These guards should be effective during threading up and normal running.

Book nipping (smashing)

Safety on hand-fed book nipping or smashing machines can only be achieved by providing guarding and safe systems of work. You need to fit adjustable access-limiting guards. These can take the form of sprung-loaded letter box guards on a horizontally moving platen or adjustable finger distancing guards on vertically moving platens.

Rounding and backing

Automatic machines should be provided with a combination of fixed and interlocked guards to prevent access to dangerous parts. On hand-fed machines access must be allowed to feed the book to the feed/rounding rollers but must be prevented during powered movement. You can prevent access to the shear trap by using sequential two-hand-controls and interlock guarding.

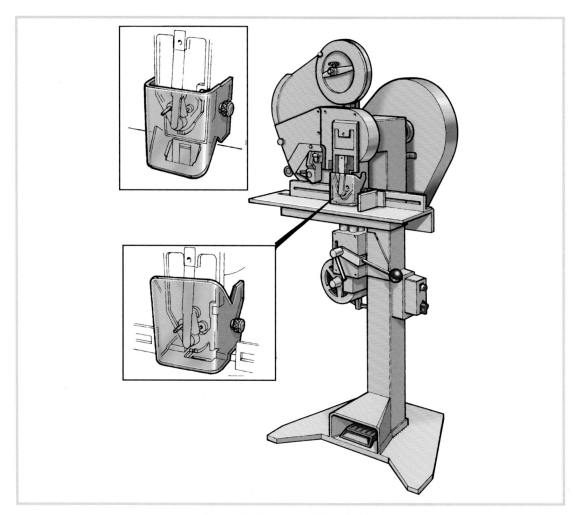

Guards for flat and saddle stitching

ACCIDENTS

Book sewing

An experienced operator crushed their index finger between the bottom platen and the book as the top platen compressed the book. No guarding had been provided.

An operator amputated the tips of two fingers while pushing books through the continuously stroking press.

Rounding and backing machines

An employee crushed his hand between the rounding rollers and backing jaw when he inadvertently started the machine cycle.

An operator bruised and lacerated his finger in the pressing plate of a rounding machine. A guard was provided but not used.

An unacceptable baling press

Baling machines

Machines used for baling wastepaper and board have caused fatal accidents and amputation injuries. Large machines typically consist of a horizontal or vertical baling chamber which is conveyor fed. These machines will have an automatic or semi-automatic bale wiring mechanism, incorporating wiring needles that pass through slots in the face of the baling ram.

Fatal accidents have also occurred when people have fallen from the conveyor into the chamber while the baler is in operation, for example when following an unsafe system of work for clearing blockages. People have been killed when they have gained access to the area behind the ram in its forward position, for running repairs, and the ram has retracted.

Amputation injuries have been caused by people gaining access to traps created by moving parts such as the ram, wire tying mechanism or wiring needles. On large machines, distributors may also constitute a danger.

At small compactors there may not be a high risk of fatality, but precautions will be needed to prevent amputations, crushing and similar major injuries.

A high standard of initial safeguarding is needed at all machines, combined with regular checks on the operation of the safety devices and maintenance. Follow safe systems of work to deal with occurrences such as blockages, and maintenance activities. Such systems should include lock-off isolation procedures for both conveyor and baler.

Initial safeguards will include a high standard of fixed and interlocked guarding, emergency stops and trip wires, fixed ladders (with hoops as appropriate) and working platforms for access to high levels of the machine.

Waste is usually loaded onto the conveyor using vehicles. Guard the edge of the conveyor or pit as far as possible and make the exposed area for loading clearly identifiable, for example by using robust overhead indicators.

Access onto conveyors should be strictly controlled by a safe system of work incorporating an effective isolation procedure. Make the means of electrical isolation readily accessible and lockable - this must isolate **both** the conveyor and the baling machine.

Fit conveyors with emergency stop devices which stop both the conveyor and the baling mechanism. Emergency stop buttons should be readily accessible from all operating stations. Emergency stop buttons or trip wires should also be provided on the inclined section of the conveyor. They can either be fitted to run up the side (preferably on both sides) or they can be positioned like goalposts horizontally across the conveyor and hung with vertical cords for ease of operation. Personal detection systems can be used as additional but not alternative safeguards.

If frequent blockages occur in the hopper above the baler then a permanent platform (at least 1.1 m below the top of the hopper)

ACCIDENTS

An operator was attempting to clear blockage in a baler. Paper was fed automatically from the shredder to the baler. When the paper level reached a magic eye the ram operated. The operator had climbed into the chute bolted to the baler. When the baler operated, his foot was badly crushed by the ram.

An employee sustained fatal crushing injuries when he became trapped by the returning ram of a large horizontal paper baling machine. He had gained access to the baling chamber via the rear of the ejector ram when the ram was in the forward position. The machine had not been isolated and the ram retracted.

An employee was killed when he fell into the baling chamber and activated the magic eye which activated the ram. The employee had been clearing a blockage at the top end of the conveyor. The machine had not been isolated.

with a fixed access ladder should be provided. If it is not possible to provide a fixed access platform, harnesses with anchorage points may be necessary in addition to the safe system of work and isolation procedure described above.

Effectively guard all openings (even small ones allowing hand access) in the vicinity of the baling chamber and the compactor/ejector ram. Access panels may be fixed in position if infrequent access is required and this should be made through a permit-to-work system incorporating an isolation procedure.

Where access is required more frequently, an interlocked guard should be provided. The standard of the interlocking required depends on the nature of the risk. If head or body access is possible then interlocking to a high standard will be required, ie guard-inhibited power interlocking (such as a key exchange system) or dual-control system interlocking with cross monitoring.

On hydraulic machines, dual control system interlocking can use a different control medium for each channel, ie one hydraulic and one electric. Where whole body access is possible, provide protection to prevent inadvertent closing of the guard panel/door while a person is inside the machine. Key exchange systems provide this protection. An equivalent standard of protection will be needed if other types of interlocking (as above) are used. Where head or body access is not required, interlocking by means of a single positively interlocked switch may be acceptable so long as it is properly maintained.

Access to the moving parts of the needles and wire-tying mechanism should be prevented by the use of fixed or interlocked guarding according to the principles described in the previous paragraphs. Needles will often pass vertically through the bale, with an access pit under the machine, but they may also be horizontal. If people have to work under the needles during maintenance, mechanical scotches should be provided to hold the needles in a safe position.

Maintenance is very important because of

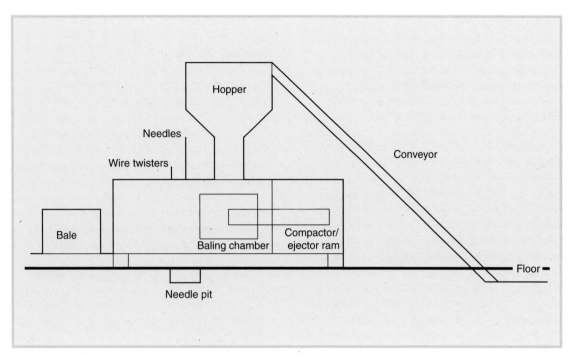

Simplified diagram of a baling machine

the heavy duty environment. Not only is it essential to ensure that safety switches/devices are regularly checked, but preventive maintenance on the plant/equipment is important to reduce the need for operator intervention.

Shredders

Machines can be hand-fed either on vertical or horizontal planes. Horizontally fed machines may have short feedside conveyors to aid the transfer of material to the cutters. Some machines may have a second conveyor to deliver the shreddings at the outrun.

Feedside access to rotary cutters

Access to the cutting rollers should be prevented by suitable distance guarding in line with BS EN 294.

For the smallest office-based machines, safety may be achieved by the use of narrow feed slots (typically narrowing to no more than 4 to 6 mm). The slots should not be in a direct vertical line with the in-running nip created by the contra-rotating cutters because of entanglement hazards to operators' hair, jewellery or clothing. Where

residual risks remain, suitable warning labels should be placed in prominent positions to alert operators of the potential hazard.

Where wastepaper etc is fed into a shredder via a top-feed chute, the chute should extend sufficiently to prevent operator hand or arm access to the rotating cutters through the chute. You can also use hinged interlocked flaps fitted with single positively operating cam switches. Opening of the flaps while the cutters are in motion should stop dangerous movement before a hand can reach the dangerous parts.

Feed chutes should be fixed in position or interlocked using positively operating switches which stop movement of the cutters before access can be gained. The type and method of interlocking should take account of cutter rundown times where applicable. Consider guard locking for machines with long cutter rundown times.

Where machines are fed horizontally using feed tables (often fitted with small integral feed conveyors), the feed table should act as a distance guard. Suitable side panelling and/or fixed or interlocked tunnel guarding should be provided to prevent access to dangerous parts from the sides of the feed table. Safety reach distances should comply with BS EN 294. Where hinged sections are provided in the guarding arrangements, these should be interlocked using positively operating interlock switches.

Outrun access to rotary cutters

Shredding machines are usually provided with a reversing drive for the rotary cutters to aid blockage removal. The reverse facility results in the otherwise out-running nips at the delivery side of the cutters becoming hazardous in-running nips. Access to these dangerous parts while they are in motion should be prevented by means of localised fixed guarding (found on some smaller machines, particularly vertically fed machines); suitable tunnel guards (fixed or interlocked); or interlocked guards. Localised fixed guards or tunnel guards should comply with BS EN 294 safety reach distances.

In exceptional circumstances reversal by means of a two-hand hold-to-run control placed out of reach of dangerous parts may be acceptable for strictly solo operating practices. Such controls should be designed to provide limited inch movement only. The controls should require simultaneous operation and comply with BS EN 60204.

Two-hand-controls are not considered acceptable if the cutters are capable of automatic reverse running. Some machines may be fitted with over current sensors which automatically reverse the direction of the cutters (and of the feed table conveyor) if the machine is overloaded. After about five seconds of reverse motion, the machine switches itself off. Provide fixed or interlocked guarding where there is a possibility of automatic reversal.

Where there are hazards after interruption of the power supply, consider interlocking methods incorporating braking and/or guard locking, for example where cutters or other dangerous parts have long rundown times. Systems should be designed to incorporate a device to either cause the hazard to be eliminated as the guard is opened (by applying a brake), or prevent the guard from being opened until the risk of injury from the hazard has passed (guard locking).

Where shredders are combined with integral baling mechanisms, any access door provided at the rear of the shredder/top of the baler should be interlocked using at least one positively operating interlock switch which prevents movement of both the shredding cutters and the baling ram as soon as the access door is opened. Hydraulic or pneumatic operated baling rams should block and dump their supply on operation of the interlock.

Provide a trip mechanism in the form of tripped access flaps or a full length trip bar as well as distance guarding where there is any possibility of an operator becoming entangled and dragged towards the cutter blade.

ACCIDENTS

An operator was feeding a paper shredder with old newspapers when her finger touched blades through an opening in the machine. The feed opening had not been restricted.

An operator severed the tip of an index finger in the cutters of a paper shredder while checking for a fault. A fixed guard had been removed from over the cutting head. Closing the electrically interlocked door of the waste sack bin had activated the cutters.

An operator lost parts of three fingers when they were sheared off by one of the compacting rams on a shredder baler machine which makes shredded newspaper into bales for animal bedding. Blockages on the machine were a regular occurrence and were frequently cleared by inserting an arm through a slot in the machinery housing while the rams were in motion. No fixed or interlocked guard was in place prior to the accident.

Acquiring machinery and other work equipment

The law

The Supply of Machinery (Safety) Regulations 1992 (amended 1994)

These Regulations impose duties on the manufacturers, suppliers and importers of new machinery and are intended to provide protection for the users of the equipment as machinery which complies with these Regulations should be safe.

The requirements of the Regulations were voluntary for new and second-hand machines from 1 January 1993 until 1 January 1995 (if they were not followed the machinery still needed to comply with the health and safety provisions in force in the United Kingdom). The requirements of the Regulations became compulsory from 1 January 1995.

Duties on manufacturers or their responsible persons

- Ensuring that the machinery or safety component satisfies the relevant essential health and safety requirements (EHSRs).

- Ensuring that an appropriate conformity assessment procedures has been carried out in accordance with the Regulations.

- Ensuring that the machinery or safety component has been issued with either a Declaration of Conformity or a Declaration of Incorporation.

- Ensuring that the machinery or safety component has been 'CE' marked to show that it satisfies the EHSRs (unless it is has a Declaration of Incorporation and is going to be incorporated into a machine or assembly of machines that will be 'CE' marked as a whole).The CE logo is below:

- Ensuring that the machinery or safety component is in fact safe.

- Carrying out research and testing to determine that the machinery is capable of being erected and put into service safely.

Duties on suppliers (where the supplier is not the manufacturer or the manufacturer's appointed responsible person)

- Ensuring that the relevant machinery or safety component is in fact safe.

Duties on users

- If you directly import any machinery (second-hand or new) from outside the European Economic Area, then the Regulations regard you as supplying the machinery to yourself and impose the duties of a supplier under the Regulations.

Examples of matters covered by the essential health and safety requirements include: principles of safety integrity; lighting; design of machinery to facilitate handling; safety and reliability of control systems; prevention of risks related to moving parts; requirements for guards and protective devices; protection from hazards (including temperature, electricity supply, static electricity, fire, explosion, noise, vibration, radiation and dusts); markings; and instructions.

The Provision and Use of Work Equipment Regulations 1992 (PUWER)

Duties on users/employers

These Regulations apply to buying or hiring new machinery. As an employer you must ensure that the work equipment you provide is suitable and safe for use.

These Regulations also require that you check that any equipment which you acquire conforms to the relevant Community Directives, eg the Supply of Machinery Regulations.

For practical purposes, you can start by ensuring that:

- Machinery supplied from 1 January 1995 comes with a copy of the manufacturer's Declaration of Conformity which states the manufacturer's name and address, the machine model and type etc.

- The machine does in fact comply with the essential health and safety requirements (EHSRS).

- The machine is accompanied by instructions for use and is 'CE' marked. Sometimes, if the machinery is going to be incorporated into other relevant machinery, eg at newspaper presses, it will come without CE marking and a Declaration of Conformity, in which case you should ask to see the manufacturer's Declaration of Incorporation. Once the equipment is assembled, the assembly as a whole will need to meet the EHSRS to be CE marked and you or the person assembling the plant will need to draw up a Declaration of Conformity.

The Health and Safety at Work etc Act 1974, section 6

This section of the Act places duties on designers, manufacturers, importers and suppliers to ensure, so far as is reasonably practicable, that any articles for use at work are safe and without risks to health and are accompanied by adequate information for use.

Word of caution

When purchasing or hiring new or second-hand machinery and work equipment, take special care to ensure that any associated risks have been assessed and that you are complying with the law. You should check that any contract deals with health and safety and that there is no misunderstanding about the condition of the machine and its guards. The law applies not only to guarding, but to other aspects which may affect health and safety, such as noise generated by machinery, solvent vapour emission, and protection against fire and explosion.

Situations may arise where 'CE' marked equipment is not entirely safe as the marking and declaration process is a self-certifying one and manufacturers or suppliers may have failed to fulfil their obligations under the regulations.

It is your duty as an employer to make sure that machinery is safe before it is brought into use. Employers are obliged by law to carry out and act upon their own assessments of health and safety risks (see 'Planning and risk assessment' in Chapter 1). Asses both new and existing machinery and bring them up to required standards.

Chapter 6
ELECTRICITY

See the References section at the back of the book for details of publications which relate to ELECTRICITY

Relevant legislation

The Electricity at Work Regulations 1989 require precautions to be taken against the risk of death or injury from electricity at work. The *Memorandum of guidance on the Electricity at Work Regulations 1989* HSR25 has further information.

Electricity can kill, even at normal mains voltage (240 V). Each year about 1000 accidents at work involving electric shock or burns are reported to HSE, around 30 of these are fatal. Fires started by poor electrical installations cause many other deaths and injuries. Explosions can be caused by electrical apparatus or static electricity igniting flammable vapours or dust.

General hazards and precautions

Check that:

- all electrical wiring is installed to a suitable standard by a competent person such as a qualified electrician. Poor workmanship can be dangerous and dangerous installations are illegal. BS 7671:1992 *Requirements for electrical installations* gives guidance on suitable standards;

- power cables to machines are insulated and protected, eg sheathed and armoured or installed in conduit. All connections should be in good condition. Switches and other equipment on distribution boards should, where appropriate, be labelled to identify the circuits they serve;

- there is a switch or isolator near each (fixed) machine to cut off power in an emergency;

- plugs, sockets and fittings are sufficiently robust and adequately protected for the working environment;

- whenever practicable, flexible cables and wires do not trail on the floor. They are more liable to damage, and may cause a tripping hazard;

- flexible cables have a suitable plug with the flex firmly clamped to stop the wires (particularly the earth) pulling out of the terminals;

- 'Christmas trees' of multi-way adapters are not used - overloading sockets in this way can cause a fire. A sufficient number of socket outlets should be provided, if

necessary, by using a multi-plug socket block;

- frayed and damaged cables are replaced completely. Join lengths in good condition only by using proper connectors or cable couplers - 'chocolate-block' connectors do not provide the strength or protection required for a joint in a flexible cable and are not suitable for this purpose;

- access is prevented to electrical danger, by keeping isolator and fuse box covers closed, secured and, it is strongly recommended, locked, with the key held by a responsible person;

- fuses, circuit breakers and other devices are correctly rated for the circuit they protect;

- rejected and poorly maintained dangerous home appliances such as fires, radios and kettles are not brought in for use at work.

Particular hazards and precautions for printing

Some precautions relate to the special conditions to be found in printing. These include:

- not using portable fan heaters or hair dryers in dark rooms or in wet conditions - they are not designed for use in such environments and unnecessary risks may result;

- making sure that the power to high pressure water jet machines used for cleaning screen printing screens is supplied through a residual current circuit breaker. This precaution will provide added protection against electrical shock;

- ensuring electrical equipment is suitably explosion protected if this is required. Flammable environments may arise in solvent storage areas and in some process areas such as in the vicinity of flexographic and gravure presses, and ink mixing areas. You may need specialist advice to choose the correct equipment. Low voltage equipment, eg 12 V, gives no protection against the ignition of flammable vapours.

Static electricity can also ignite flammable vapours. This is a particular problem in flexographic and gravure printing. Important precautions include:

- the use by operators of antistatic footwear to prevent the build up of electrostatic charges which might cause a spark. Where this is a hazard, operators also need to avoid wearing clothing made of man-made fibre (this can have the additional advantage of reducing the severity of burns in the event of a fire);

- the use of closed metal containers when carrying flammable liquids such as solvents;

- the bonding and earthing of metalwork as necessary to prevent accumulation of static where flammable liquids such as solvents are transferred by pipe or poured.

Inspection and maintenance

All electrical equipment, wiring installations (including battery sets), their connections (including fixed items of machinery) and portable electric tools must be maintained so far as is reasonably practicable to prevent danger. You will need to carry out visual inspections and repair and back this up with testing as necessary - how often will depend on the equipment you use and where you use it. See the *Memorandum of Guidance on the Electricity at Work Regulations 1989*. You may find it helpful to keep records of inspection and combined inspection and testing.

Take suspect or faulty equipment out of use, label it 'DO NOT USE' and, where appropriate, remove the plug and keep it secure until checked by a competent person. In addition, have a system for your employees to report to you any damage or defects they discover.

Don't overlook hired or borrowed tools or equipment like floor polishers which may be used after the premises have closed.

Check that residual current circuit breakers work by operating the test button regularly, in accordance with the manufacturer's advice. It has been known for these devices to fail if the contacts fuse together.

Anyone carrying out electrical work must be competent to do it safely. This may mean bringing in outside contractors. If you do need to use electrical contractors you can use those who belong to an organisation which checks their work such as the National Inspection Council for Electrical Installation Contracting (NICEIC). Your own staff must also be competent if you do the work in-house.

If you have equipment for use in flammable atmospheres, make sure that special maintenance requirements for explosion-protected equipment have been written down and that someone with sufficient training is made responsible for carrying out the work. The manufacturer of the equipment should be able to give you advice on this.

No-one should be allowed to work on or near exposed live equipment, unless it is unavoidable, they are properly trained, and suitable precautions are taken. If in doubt, ask your enforcing authority for advice.

Electric shock

Would you know what to do if someone received an electric shock? Knowing what to do should be part of your emergency procedures and first-aid arrangements. Think about displaying a copy of the 'Electric shock placard' which shows you what to do (see below and the References section).

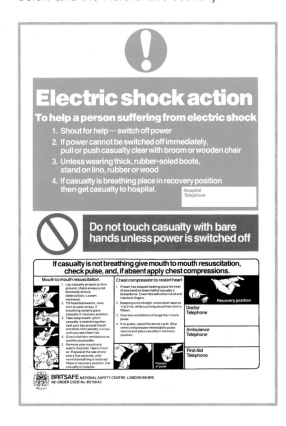

ACCIDENTS

A minder received an electric shock when he touched a metal table beside his machine. A damaged cable running along the floor was in contact with the table, making it electrically live. The man was off work for one week, but the accident could have had far more serious consequences.

A manager was killed while using a pressure washer. An electrical fault on the washer made its frame and lance live at 240 V. Earthing was inadequate and no residual current device was fitted in the supply.

A 16-year-old trainee printer received a 240 V electric shock and burns to his fingers when he touched a switch, the cover to which had been removed and not replaced.

Chapter 7

FIRE AND EXPLOSION

▪ ▪ ▪ ▪ ▪ ▪ ▪ ▪ ▪ ▪ ▪ ▪

See the References section at the back of the book for details of publications which relate to FIRE AND EXPLOSION

Relevant legislation

Requirements for **process** fire precautions can be found in the following pieces of legislation:

- Health and Safety at Work etc Act 1974

- Management of Health and Safety at Work Regulations 1992

- Workplace (Health Safety and Welfare) Regulations 1992

- Provision and Use of Work Equipment Regulations 1992

- Highly Flammable Liquids and Liquefied Petroleum Gases Regulations 1972

- The Equipment and Protective Systems for Use in Potentially Explosive Atmospheres Regulations 1996

- Electricity at Work Regulations 1989

- Petroleum (Consolidation) Act 1928

Several hundred fires occur every year in the printing industry. There have also been a number of explosions. In some incidents people have been killed or injured; in many others there has been extensive damage to buildings, equipment and materials.

Explosions can occur at dryers used in association with flexographic presses and when blanket washing on heat-set web offset presses. They occur because flammable substances, such as solvents, blanket wash etc, if not used or stored correctly, can form an explosive mixture with air.

General fire precautions

Your local fire authority, rather than HSE, will give you advice on this. You may need a fire certificate for your building - this will depend on the kind of business you run and the number of people employed in your building. The main pieces of legislation are the Fire Precautions Act 1971 and the Fire Precautions (Workplace) Regulations 1997.

A fire certificate is generally required if more than 20 people are at work in the premises at any one time or if more than 10 people are at work at any one time elsewhere than on the ground floor. A fire certificate may also be required if explosive or highly flammable materials are stored or used either in or under the premises.

You need to check that:

- everyone knows what to do in case of fire. Display clear instructions and have a fire drill periodically;

- people know how to raise the alarm and use the extinguishers where appropriate;

- suitable arrangements are in place for calling the fire brigade to any suspected outbreak of fire;

- enough exits are provided for everyone to get out easily;

- fire doors and escape routes are provided which are clearly marked and unobstructed;

- fire escape doors can be opened easily from the inside whenever anyone is on the premises - don't forget 'out of hours' working;

- fire doors are never wedged open - they are there to stop smoke and flames spreading;

- if a wall is meant to be fire-resisting, it has no holes or gaps (eg around pipework) and the wall continues above any false ceiling;

- fire alarms are checked regularly and work. Can they be heard everywhere over normal background noise?

- enough fire extinguishers are provided and are of the right type (and properly serviced) to deal promptly with small outbreaks.

Process fire precautions

Main fire hazards

The main fire hazards are:

- poor housekeeping/accumulation of waste material;

- handling/storage of flammable liquids, solids and gases, eg solvents in litho and letterpress printing;

- heating and drying equipment, eg ultraviolet curing units, gravure dryers;

- poorly maintained or unsuitable electrical equipment;

- frictional heat, eg from hot bearings;

- frictional sparks, eg from using tools;

- electrostatic sparks;

- welding and cutting;

- smoking materials;

- arson and horseplay.

The fire triangle

The fire triangle can be used to consider fire precautions. Each point of the triangle represents one of the three elements essential for fire: fuel, oxygen and a source of ignition. Fire can be prevented by avoiding all three of these elements existing simultaneously.

FUEL

OXYGEN   IGNITION

For example, the safe storage and use of combustible materials such as paper, board and inks is important to ensure that they do not come into contact with potential sources of ignition, eg hot surfaces, static electricity, cigarettes, battery chargers.

Highly flammable liquid (HFL) stores should have suitable markings, ventilation and spillage retention

Flammable liquids

Special precautions are needed for flammable liquids. A highly flammable liquid (HFL) is one with a flashpoint of less than 32°C. A flammable liquid is one with a flashpoint between 32°C and 55°C.

Highly flammable liquids must be kept in suitable containers in:

- a safe position in the open air (where necessary, protected from direct sunlight); or

- in a storeroom that is in a safe position; or

- in a fire-resisting store; or

- if the total quantity is less than 50 litres it may be kept in the workroom in a suitable fire-resisting cupboard or bin.

All storerooms, cupboards or bins should be marked to indicate the nature of their contents, eg 'highly flammable'. Storerooms should also have adequate ventilation. All storage facilities should have spillage retention, eg bunding.

It is recommended that flammable liquids are stored in a similar manner to highly flammable liquids.

HFL storage containers need to be maintained, correctly sited and protected from vehicle damage to remain effective

Some of the key steps for the safe use and control of highly flammable and flammable liquids are to:

- minimise the amount kept at the workplace;

- dispense and use them in a safe place with adequate natural or mechanical ventilation;

- keep containers closed, eg use safety containers with self-closing lids and caps;

- contain spillages, eg by dispensing over a tray and having absorbent material handy;

- ensure that electrical equipment is suitable, eg intrinsically safe or flameproof where appropriate;

- control ignition sources, eg naked flames and sparks, and make sure that 'no smoking' rules are obeyed, especially when spraying highly flammable liquids;

- keep contaminated material, eg rags containing isopropylalcohol (IPA) in a marked, lidded, metal bin which is emptied regularly;

- prevent the accumulation of combustible materials such as wastepaper in areas in which highly flammable and flammable liquids are kept or used;

- get rid of waste safely, eg burn rubbish in a suitable container well away from buildings. Have fire extinguishers on hand. Never burn aerosol cans or 'brighten' fires with flammable liquids.

Fire risk management

Management arrangements are needed to ensure that fire risks are adequately controlled. These should include arrangements to ensure that:

- the risk of fire occurring is reduced to the absolute minimum;

- the risk of fire spreading is minimised, eg by the separation of combustible materials;

- everyone is able to reach a safe place beyond the building through their own unaided efforts.

It might be appropriate to designate a senior member of the management team to have specific responsibility for fire risk management and staff training.

A thorough fire survey is likely to be necessary in order to properly assess the fire risks from materials and processes, and the arrangements that are needed in the event of fire breaking out. A fire action plan can then be produced to deal with the matters which have been identified. An example of an action plan is given on page 118.

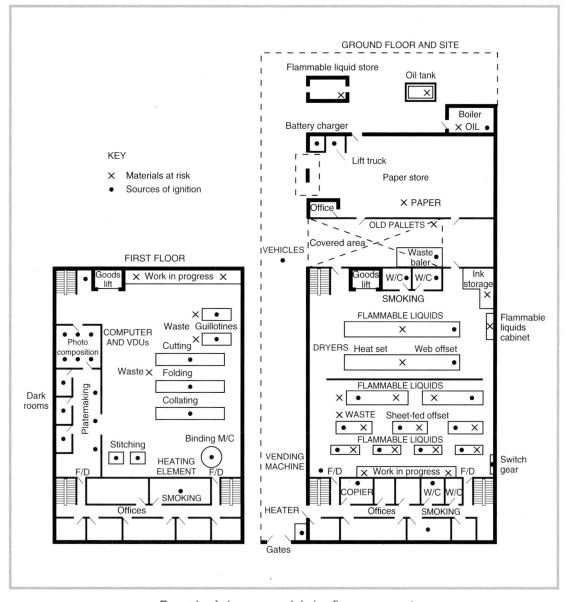

Example of plan prepared during fire assessment

Action plan for fire risk management

Managing Director decides to minimise fire risks

Senior Manager appointed to consider improvements needed to reduce fire risks

Control programme initiated

Combustible/flammable materials identified

Arrangements in the event of fire and fire risks from materials/processes assessed and improvements identified, in consultation with safety representatives

Adequate fire precautions provided
Fire risks controlled

Adequate supervision provided and employees informed, instructed and trained
Fire evacuation drills held at regular intervals

Standards monitored by regular management inspections, inspections by safety representatives and thorough investigation of any incidents - corrective action taken

Report at defined intervals to senior management and review

Explosion risks in blanket wash systems

Serious explosions have occurred at blanket wash systems at heat-set web offset printing. Explosions have occurred in dryers on web offset printing lines when the web has transferred blanket wash solvent into the dryer and the concentration of solvent in the dryer has exceeded the lower flammable limit (LFL).

The design and operation of heat-set dryers are such that ignition of solvent vapour is almost inevitable if a concentration above the LFL is formed within the dryers. Standards have been devised to ensure the safe operation of this type of plant. You will need to check that your equipment has been designed with safety in mind.

Check that the dryers have:

- suitable gas safety features on gas-fired dryers, including safety shut-off valves, ignition systems, flame failure devices and purging arrangements;

- adequate explosion relief doors or panels on the dryer. This protection is critical if the damage caused by an explosion is to be minimised. The area and weight of explosion relief panels need to be carefully calculated, so that they are effective if an explosion occurs;

- sufficient exhaust ventilation from the dryer, so that under all operating conditions the concentration of solvent in the dryer does not exceed 25% of the LFL. As failure of the exhaust system may have critical effects, it should be monitored so that any reduction in the air flow below pre-determined levels will automatically and safely shut down the fuel supply to the dryer, the blanket wash system and the printed web. It should also activate a visible and audible alarm.

Check the automatic blanket wash systems for the following:

- The monitoring and control devices automatically ensure that in all circumstances the overall solvent concentration in the dryer does not exceed 25% of the LFL.

FIRES IN THE PRINTING INDUSTRY

Fire in reel store

Three employees died in a fire in the reel store of a printing factory. The fire started in some reels of paper at one end of the reel store in this single-storey factory. There was no fire separation between the reel storage area and the production area. Shortly after the fire was first discovered there was a sudden rapid spread of fire (flashover) across the top of reels of paper and the whole building rapidly filled with smoke. The roof collapsed within minutes.

Horseplay with flammable thinners

A 17-year-old apprentice died of extensive burns after an initiation ceremony in which 2 litres of flammable thinners were poured on his clothing. The victim was changing his soaked clothing in a toilet cubicle when some matches were lit. The apprentice was engulfed in flames and died three weeks later of burns which covered 80% of his body.

Arson

On arriving at a warehouse just after midnight, the fire brigade found a timber tea chest or pallet on fire outside double timber doors in an alleyway adjacent to the seven-storey building. The doors were burning and fire was spreading under the doors into a stairwell. The first and second floors were also alight. Fire spread was rapid due to the type of storage and unprotected stairways in the warehouse areas. The entire seven-storey warehouse was severely damaged.

Ignition of toluene vapour

A printer was off work for six weeks after receiving severe burns to his right hand when a static discharge occurred as he was using a toluene-soaked rag to clean the doctor blade of a gravure printing press. It is thought that an earlier modification to a cover at the doctor blade had reduced the extraction system's ability to remove toluene vapours given off by the printing ink. Anti-static footwear was not in use.

Smoking near flammable solvent

An employee sustained burns to his face and hair as he cleaned a roller washing machine with flammable solvent while smoking. After the incident all staff were instructed not to smoke in the room where the machine was located and 'no smoking' signs were posted up.

Further detailed guidance on fire safety can be found in the booklet *Fire safety in the printing industry*.

- The solvent or ink used in the system should be the same as that which was used when the system was commissioned. Different solvents may have different flammable limits, and a change of solvent may result in dangerous conditions. Check with the supplier of the system before making any changes.

- The blanket wash supplier has provided information about the LFL for the solvent used, in relation to the typical dryer operating temperatures (160-260°C).

- The quantity of solvent applied to the blanket cylinders is metered, and is the minimum necessary. This volume will have been set during commissioning. Check that unauthorised access to the controlling mechanism is prevented.

- The manual application of additional solvent is strictly prohibited. Safety will be compromised if the amount of solvent reaching the dryer is greater than that expected by the designer of the system.

- If blanket wash drip-trays are used, care is taken so that they do not overflow and allow the web to take excess solvent into the dryer.

- Adequate written information has been provided by the supplier about the conditions under which the system has been commissioned, operational limitations, the safety devices, the results of commissioning and necessary maintenance requirements.

- Managers, operators and assistants are adequately trained in the explosion hazard associated with blanket washing and in the necessary precautionary measures.

In addition, when blanket washing by hand, remember that it is important to:

- remove or break the web before the dryer, and don't use it as a wiper;

- keep the quantity of solvent applied to a minimum.

Explosion risks in flexo and gravure

Precautions are necessary to prevent the risk of explosion in dryers used in flexo and gravure printing. These include:

- the use of suitably explosion-protected electrical and non-electrical, eg pneumatic, apparatus/equipment on the press and in any of the surrounding area where an explosive atmosphere might foreseeably occur, so as not to present a risk of ignition;

- the use of appropriate measures to prevent the build-up of static electricity on the web, plant and personnel, to prevent risk of static igniting vapours that may be present, eg anti-static footwear and earthing of ink containers;

- the use of appropriate fire detection and extinguishing systems;

- operation of the dryer so that the solvent concentration in it does not exceed 25% LFL (unless the dryer was specifically designed to operate above this level), with monitoring and control devices to ensure safety if solvent levels rise unacceptably;

- the provision of explosion relief panels on the dryer and on large scale ductwork;

- interlocking of the movement of the printed web with the operation of the exhaust ventilation.

For guidance on these and other precautionary measures see the booklet *Fire safety in the printing industry*.

ACCIDENT

A dryer at a gravure press was substantially damaged by an explosion, although employees fortunately escaped injury. The web had dipped into a coating duct when the press was stationary. Excess solvent was therefore carried into the dryer when the plant started up. The coating was already being applied to the substrate at a weight in excess of the parameters specified by the dryer manufacturer. The web dip-in then easily caused the LFL to be exceeded in the dryer. Explosion relief on the dryer was badly designed and did not fully protect the plant from structural damage. The fire following the explosion caused further damage.

Chapter 8

MAINTENANCE

■ ■ ■ ■ ■ ■ ■ ■ ■ ■ ■ ■

See the References section at the back of the book for details of publications which relate to MAINTENANCE

Relevant legislation

- Provision and Use of Work Equipment Regulations 1992

- Workplace (Health, Safety and Welfare) Regulations 1992

- Health and Safety at Work etc Act 1974

- Control of Substances Hazardous to Health Regulations 1994

- Pressure Systems and Transportable Gas Containers Regulations 1989

- Electricity at Work Regulations 1989

- Lifting Operations and Lifting Equipment Regulations 1998

What needs maintenance?

All buildings, equipment and plant need to be maintained in good working order and in good repair so as to prevent any dangerous situations occurring.

The law contains some specific requirements for maintenance such as periodic testing and/or thorough examination. For example:

- lifting chains and ropes - generally every six months (although this will be dependent on the findings of an appropriate risk assessment);

- lifts and hoists - generally every six months (although this will be dependent on the findings of an appropriate risk assessment);

- cranes - generally every 12 months (although this will be dependent on the findings of an appropriate risk assessment);

- steam boilers/air receivers and pressure systems - in accordance with your competent person's written scheme for examination of pressure vessels;

- local exhaust ventilation - minimum every 14 months (see the General Approved Code of Practice for the COSHH Regulations 1994, listed in the References for Chapter 4).

Periodic tests such as these need to be carried out by a competent person - this may be your insurance engineer.

Other examples of required and industry recommended inspections include:

- inspection of personal protective equipment, eg hearing protection;

- weekly inspection of scaffolds;

- monthly examination of breathing apparatus/rescue equipment;

- monthly/six-monthly examination of guillotine safety devices (see the booklet *Safety at power-operated paper-cutting guillotines*).

To be effective these inspections/ examinations will need to be carried out by specially approved, trained and responsible people.

Examples of other regular inspections and checks include:

- daily inspection of guards and safety mechanisms by machine operators;

- regular visual inspections of electrical equipment at appropriate intervals. Practical experience/manufacturer's guidance will help to determine the frequency at which inspections by a competent person are necessary (eg quarterly/annually). This should be backed up by a system including checks by the users and appropriate testing. Keeping records will help to determine the frequencies. Guidance is contained in the publication *Maintaining portable and transportable electrical equipment* (HSG107).

Routine lubrication, service and overhaul activities might include:

- cleaning of floors and machinery access platforms/walkways (eg flexopresses);

- annual servicing of fire extinguishers.

Be guided by the manufacturer's recommendations when working out your own maintenance schedules for items such as vehicles, lift trucks, ventilation plant, ladders, portable electrical equipment, protective clothing and equipment and machine guards. Check the legal requirements, especially for examinations by a competent person.

Safety during maintenance work

During maintenance work, conditions are very different from those normally encountered, and new hazards may be introduced. It is essential that everyone concerned is aware of the hazards and of the correct precautions.

Appropriate personal protective equipment may be needed during maintenance activities, eg overalls, protective footwear and headwear. Suitable gloves may be needed if handling inky machine parts, eg changing ink rollers on a litho press using UV inks.

Safety during maintenance activities can be achieved by using isolation, lock-off and permit-to-work procedures. Generally speaking, simple isolation procedures may be suitable for minor maintenance work and formal lock-off procedures for more major maintenance work.

You will need permit-to-work procedures for complicated activities where lock-off and

ACCIDENTS

An experienced guillotine operator lost four fingers on one hand when a repeat stroke occurred. The machine had not been maintained, its brake was worn and oily and the automatic sweepaway guard did not operate to its full extent. The PIAC recommended examinations would have identified these faults early enough to prevent an accident.

A machine operator had his right index finger severely crushed while cleaning the ink rollers of a bag printing machine. The interlock for the hinged guard had worked loose and he inadvertently depressed the start button. Daily checking and maintenance of the safety device would have prevented the accident. Shrouding of

the start button would have prevented accidental operation of the button.

The operator of a three-knife trimmer received an electric shock while picking up a knife from the floor and resting one hand on the machine. Investigation by an electrician revealed a faulty earth connection. Regular planned maintenance would have identified this defect.

An experienced fitter was killed while working at the feed end of a paper cutting and creasing machine when the operator, who did not see him, started up the machine. There was no safe system for maintenance work and the machine had not been isolated.

isolation procedures are not likely to be adequate. Consider each maintenance activity, assess the risks and decide which is the most appropriate way of ensuring safety.

Isolation procedures usually comprise the following:

- switch off;

- disconnect plug;

- switch off isolator;

- tag isolator.

Lock-off procedures usually involve the following steps:

- isolate the machine from the main supply by locking off the power;

- use a safety lock with only one key;

- use a multiple hasp where several people are working so each can fit their own lock.

- put a warning notice on the isolator.

Permit-to-work procedures will normally be needed for activities such as the following:

- entry into vessels, confined spaces or machines;

- hot work which may cause explosion or fire;

- construction work or employment of contractors;

- mechanical or electrical work requiring isolation of the power source, eg before working inside large machines;

- work on plant, mixers, boilers etc which must be cut off from the possible entry of fumes, gas, liquids or steam.

A permit-to-work document should state exactly what work is to be done, by whom and who is responsible. It should also state when the work is to be carried out, the precautions which need to be taken and which parts are safe. A permit-to-work document needs to be part of a carefully thought out permit-to-work procedure designed to ensure that safety precautions are understood and implemented at all stages.

HOW TO OBTAIN PUBLICATIONS

HSE Publications

HSE priced and free publications (including many of those produced by PIAC) are available from HSE Books; see back cover for details.

PIAC Bulletins

These are available from:

Paper and Printing NIG
Health and Safety Executive
3 East Grinstead House
London Road
East Grinstead
West Sussex
RH19 1RR

Tel: 01342 334200
Fax: 01342 334222

Stationery Office (formerly HMSO) publications

Copies of the acts, regulations and other Stationery Office (formerly HMSO) publications mentioned in this guide are available from:

The Publications Centre,
PO Box 276
London SW8 5DT
Telephone orders 0171 873 9090
General enquiries 0171 873 0011
Fax orders 0171 873 8200
(Mail, fax and telephone orders only)

and all HMSO bookshops

British Standards

British Standards are available from:

BSI Sales and Customer Services
389 Chiswick High Road
London W4 4AL
Tel: 0181 996 7000
Fax: 0181 996 7001

REFERENCES

■ ■ ■ ■ ■ ■ ■ ■ ■ ■ ■

IMPORTANT MACHINERY STANDARDS

These are available from BSI, see 'How to obtain publications'.

The current EN Standards give specifications for new machines. However, some of the precautions may be relevant to existing machines when it is reasonably practicable to fit them.

BS EN 294: 1992 *Safety of machinery: safety distances to prevent danger zones being reached by the upper limbs*

BS EN 953: 1997 *Safety of machinery: general requirements for the design and construction of guards (fixed, movable)*

EN 1010: 1998 (Draft) *Safety of machinery: safety requirements for the design and construction of printing and paper converting machinery*

EN 1088: 1996 *Safety of machinery: interlocking devices associated with guards - principles for design and selection*

BS 5304: 1998 *British standard code of practice for safety of machinery*

BS EN 60204: 1993 *Safety of machinery: electrical equipment of machines. Part 1 Specification for general requirements*

BS EN 292: 1991 *Safety of machinery: basic concepts, general principles for design. Part 1: 1991 Basic terminology, methodology. Part 2 Technical principles and specifications* Amended A1 1995

BS EN 1050: 1997 *Safety of machinery: principles for risk assessment*

BS EN 811: 1997 *Safety of machinery: safety distances to prevent danger zones being reached by the lower limbs*

BS EN 349: 1993 *Safety of machinery: minimum gaps to avoid crushing parts of the human body*

BS 7671: 1992 *Requirements for electrical installations*

BS EN 60825: 1994 *Safety of laser products Part 1: Equipment classification, requirements and user's guide*

BS EN 352: 1993 *Hearing protectors - safety requirements and testing Part 1: Ear-muffs. Part 2: Ear-plugs. Part 3: 1997 Ear-muffs attached to an industrial safety helmet*

BS EN 166: 1996 *Personal eye-protection - specifications*

BS EN 345: 1993 *Safety footwear for professional use*

BS EN 346: 1993 *Protective footwear for professional use*

BS EN 61496: 1998 *Electrosensitive protective equipment - Part 2: Particular requirements for an ESPE using an active octo-electronic protective device for the sensing function* (currently being prepared)

CHAPTER 1 MANAGING HEALTH AND SAFETY

HSG65 *Successful health and safety management* (second edition) HSE Books 1997 ISBN 0 7176 1276 7

HSG96 *The cost of accidents at work* (second edition) HSE Books 1997 ISBN 0 7176 1343 7

L1 *A guide to the Health and Safety at Work etc Act 1974* (fifth edition) HSE Books 1992 ISBN 0 7176 0441 1

L21 *Management of health and safety at work. Management of Health and Safety at Work Regulations 1992. Approved Code of Practice* HSE Books 1992 ISBN 0 7176 0412 8

Poster: Health and Safety Law: What you should know HMSO 1989 ISBN 0 11 701424 9

Writing your health and safety policy statement HSE Books 1989 ISBN 0 7176 0424 1

IACL14* *Safety policies in the printing industry* HSE Books 1994

HSC2* *Health and Safety at Work etc Act: The Act Outlined* HSE Books 1990

HSC6* *Writing a safety policy statement: advice to employers* HSE Books 1990

HSC8* *Safety committees: Guidance to employers whose employees are not members of recognised trade unions* HSE Books 1990

HSC13* *Health and safety regulations: a short guide* HSE Books 1995

L87 *Safety representatives and safety committees* (the Brown Book) Third edition HSE Books 1996 ISBN 0 7176 1220 1

HSE4* *A short guide to the Employer's Liability (Compulsory Insurance) Act* HSE Books 1976

HSE34* *HSE and you* HSE Books 1996

HSE35* *HSE: working with employers* HSE Books 1996

MISC071* *Health and safety in small firms* HSE Books 1996

INDG132* *Five steps to successful health and safety management: special help for directors and managers* HSE Books 1992

INDG163 *Five steps to risk assessment: a step by step guide to a safer, healthier workplace* HSE Books 1995 Single copies available free, multiple copies in priced packs ISBN 0 7176 0904 9

HSG137 *Health risk management: A practical guide for managers in small and medium-sized enterprises* HSE Books 1995 ISBN 0 7176 0905 7

MISC069* *Good health is good business: employers' guide* HSE Books 1996

INDS29* *Introducing competent persons: Pressure Systems and Transportable Gas Containers Regulations 1989* HSE Books 1991

INDG232* *Consulting employees on health and safety: A guide to the law* HSE Books 1996

HSE31 *Everyone's guide to RIDDOR 95* HSE Books 1996 Single copies free, multiple copies in priced packs ISBN 0 7176 1077 2

L74 *First aid at work. The Health and Safety at First-Aid at Work Regulations 1981. Approved Code of Practice and guidance* HSE Books 1997 ISBN 0 7176 1050 0

INDG214 *First aid at work: your questions answered* HSE Books 1997 Single copies free, multiple copies in priced packs ISBN 0 7176 1074 8

L54 *Managing construction for health and safety. Construction (Design and Management) Regulations 1994. Approved Code of Practice* HSE Books 1995 ISBN 0 7176 0792 5

INDG220 *A guide to the Construction (Health, Safety and Welfare) Regulations 1996* HSE Books 1996 Single copies free, multiple copies in priced packs ISBN 0 7176 1161 2

CHAPTER 2 TRAINING

INDG213 *Five steps to information, instruction and training* HSE Books 1996 Single copies free, multiple copies in priced packs ISBN 0 7176 1235 X

PIAC guidance

IACL66* *Training for health and safety in the printing industry* HSE Books 1992

* Those publications marked with an asterisk in this References section are free

Printing industry: health and safety training package HSE Books 1998
ISBN 0 7176 1481 6

CHAPTER 3 WORKPLACE AND TRANSPORT SAFETY

L24 *Workplace health, safety and welfare. Workplace (Health, Safety and Welfare) Regulations 1992. Approved Code of Practice and guidance* HSE Books 1992
ISBN 0 7176 0413 6

COP 26 *Rider-operated lift trucks: operator training: Approved Code of Practice and supplementary guidance* HSE Books 1988
ISBN 0 7176 0474 8

HSG6 *Safety in working with lift trucks* HSE Books 1993 ISBN 0 11 886395 9

HSG76 *Health and safety in retail and wholesale warehouses* HSE Books 1992
ISBN 0 11 885731 2

HSG136 *Workplace transport safety: guidance for employers* HSE Books 1995
ISBN 0 7176 0935 9

INDG199 *Managing vehicle safety at the workplace* HSE Books 1995 Single copies free, multiple copies in priced packs
ISBN 0 7176 0982 0

INDG244* *Workplace health safety and welfare: a short guide for managers* HSE Books 1997

L22 *Work equipment. Provision and Use of Work Equipment Regulations 1992. Guidance on regulations* HSE Books 1992 ISBN 0 7176 0414 4 (Due to be revised later in 1998)

L23 *Manual handling. Manual Handling Operations Regulations 1992. Guidance on regulations* HSE Books 1992
ISBN 0 7176 0411 X

L26 *Display screen equipment work. Health and Safety (Display Screen Equipment) Regulations 1992. Guidance on regulations* HSE Books 1992 ISBN 0 7176 0410 1

INDG187* *Asbestos dust - the hidden killer. Are you at risk? Essential advice for building maintenance, repair and refurbishment workers* HSE Books 1995

INDG107 *Asbestos and you* HSE Books 1996 Single copies free, multiple copies in priced packs ISBN 0 7176 1241 4

PABIAC guidance

Handling reels of paper and board HSE Books 1984 ISBN 0 11 883741 9

CHAPTER 4 HEALTH RISKS

Hazardous substances

HSG97 *A step by step guide to COSHH Assessment* HSE Books 1993
ISBN 0 11 886379 7

EH40/97 *Occupational Exposure Limits* (Revised annually) HSE Books 1997
ISBN 0 7176 1315 1

L5 *General COSHH ACOP and Carcinogens ACOP and Biological Agents ACOP. Control of Substances Hazardous to Health Regulations 1994* HSE Books 1997 ISBN 0 7176 1308 9

PIAC guidance

Control of health hazards in screen printing HSE Books 1988 ISBN 0 11 883973 X

Chemical safety in the printing industry HSE Books 1995 ISBN 0 7176 0846 8

Safe use of isocyanates in printing and laminating HSE Books 1997
ISBN 0 7176 1312 7

Safety in the use of inks, varnishes and lacquers cured by ultraviolet light or electron beam techniques HSE Books 1993
ISBN 0 11 882045 1

PIAC Bulletin* *Occupational asthma* 1996

IACL85* *Solvent safety in printing* HSE Books 1993

IACL96* *The supply of chemicals to printers* HSE Books 1996

Noise

INDG193 *Health surveillance in noisy industries* HSE Books 1995 Single copies free, multiple copies in priced packs ISBN 0 7176 0933 2

INDG200 *Ear protection in noisy firms - employer's duties explained* HSE Books 1995 Single copies free, multiple copies in priced packs ISBN 0 7176 0924 3

MS26 *A guide to audiometric testing programmes* HSE Books 1995
ISBN 0 7176 0942 1

L3 *Noise at work. Noise guide No 1: Legal duties of employers to prevent damage to hearing. Noise guide No 2: Legal duties of designers, manufacturers, importers and suppliers to prevent damage to hearing. The Noise at Work Regulations 1989* HSE Books 1996 ISBN 0 7176 0454 3

HSG56 *Noise at work: Noise guides Nos 3-8: Noise assessment, information and control* HSE Books 1990 ISBN 0 11 885430 5

INDG75 *Introducing the Noise at Work Regulations: a brief guide to the requirements for controlling noise at work* HSE Books 1996 Single copies free, multiple copies in priced packs ISBN 0 7176 0961 8

INDG99 *Noise at work: advice to employees* HSE Books 1995 Single copies free, multiple copies in priced packs ISBN 0 7176 0962 6

HSG138 *Sound solutions: techniques to reduce noise at work* HSE Books 1995 ISBN 0 7176 0791 7

PIAC guidance

Noise reduction at web-fed presses HSE Books 1988 ISBN 0 11 883972 1

Noise reduction at buckle-folding machines HSE Books 1986 ISBN 0 11 883849 0

Manual handling

L23 *Manual handling. Manual Handling Operations Regulations 1992. Guidance on Regulations* HSE Books 1992 ISBN 0 7176 0411 X

INDG143 *Getting to grips with manual handling: a short guide for employers* HSE Books 1993 Single copies free, multiple copies in priced packs ISBN 0 7176 0966 9

HSG60 *Work-related upper limb disorders: a guide to prevention* HSE Books 1990 ISBN 0 7176 0475 6

HSG115 *Manual handling: solutions you can handle* HSE Books 1994 ISBN 0 7176 0693 7

HSG121 *A pain in your workplace: ergonomic problems and solutions* HSE Books 1994 ISBN 0 7176 0668 6

Upper limb disorders: Assessing the risks INDG171 HSE Books 1995 Single copies free, multiple copies in priced packs ISBN 0 7176 0751 8

PIAC guidance

IACL91 *Work-related upper limb disorders in the printing industry* HSE Books 1994

Safe handling of materials in the printing industry HSE Books 1988 ISBN 0 11 883983 7 (under revision)

Other publications

IACL65A* *Monitoring for health and safety in print: a guide to management action* HSE Books 1992

INDG240* *Don't mix it: A guide for employers on alcohol at work* HSE Books 1996

HSG116 *Stress at work: a guide for employers* HSE Books 1995 ISBN 07176 0733 X

HSG122 *New and expectant mothers at work: A guide for employers* HSE Books 1994 ISBN 0 7176 0826 3

INDG91 *Drug abuse at work* HSE Books 1990 Single copies free, multiple copies in priced packs ISBN 0 7176 0873 5

INDG63 *Passive smoking at work* HSE Books 1995 Single copies free, multiple copies in priced packs ISBN 0 7176 0882 4

L74 *First aid at work. The Health and Safety at First-Aid at Work Regulations 1981. Approved Code of Practice and guidance* HSE Books 1997 ISBN 0 7176 1050 0

HSG70 *The control of legionellosis including legionnaires' disease* HSE Books 1993 ISBN 0 7176 0451 9

HSG37 *Introduction to local exhaust ventilation* HSE Books 1993 ISBN 0 7176 1001 2

HSG54 *The maintenance, examination and testing of local exhaust ventilation* HSE Books 1990 ISBN 0 11 885438 0

L25 *Personal protective equipment at work. Personal Protective Equipment at Work Regulations 1992. Guidance on regulations* HSE Books 1992 ISBN 0 7176 0415 2

L26 *Display screen equipment work. Health and Safety (Display Screen Equipment) Regulations 1992. Guidance on regulations* HSE Books 1992 ISBN 0 7176 0410 1

INDG133* *Selecting a health and safety consultant* HSE Books 1992

PM29 *Electrical risks from steam/water pressure cleaners* HSE Books 1995 ISBN 0 7176 0813 1

PIAC guidance

IACL28* *Humidifier fever in the printing industry* HSE Books 1989

Laser safety in printing HSE Books 1990 ISBN 0 11 885436 4

CHAPTER 5 PROCESS SAFETY

L22 *Work equipment. Provision and use of Work Equipment Regulations 1992. Guidance on regulations* HSE Books 1992 ISBN 0 7176 0414 4 (due to be revised later in 1998)

HSG90 *VDUs: An easy guide to the Regulations* HSE Books 1994 ISBN 0 7176 0735 6

Supply of Machinery (Safety) Regulations 1992 SI 1992/3073 HMSO 1992 ISBN 0 11 025719 7 and *Supply of Machinery (Safety) Amendment Regulations 1994* SI 1994/2063 HMSO 1994 ISBN 0 11 045063 9

HSE Information Sheet* *The Supply of Machinery (Safety) Regulations* HSE Books 1992

PIAC guidance

PIAC Bulletin* *Sheet-fed litho presses: preventing cleaning accidents* 1996

Safety at power-operated paper-cutting guillotines HSE Books 1988 ISBN 0 11 885460 7

CHAPTER 6 ELECTRICITY

HSR25 *Memorandum of guidance on the Electricity at Work Regulations 1989* HSE Books 1989 ISBN 0 7176 0422 5 (due to be revised in 1998)

HSG85 *Electricity at work: safe working practices* HSE Books 1993 ISBN 0 7176 0 442 X (due to be revised in 1998)

INDG231* *Electrical safety and you* HSE Books 1996 Single copies free, multiple copies in priced packs ISBN 0 7176 1207 4

PM29 *Electrical risks from steam/water pressure cleaners* HSE Books 1995 ISBN 0 7176 0813 1

INDG68(rev)* *Do you use a steam/water pressure cleaner? You could be in for a shock* HSE Books 1997

Electric shock placard MISC 046 HSE Books 1996 ISBN 0 7176 1123 X

CHAPTER 7 FIRE AND EXPLOSION

INDG227* *Safe working with flammable substances* HSE Books 1996 Single copies free, multiple copies in priced packs ISBN 0 7176 1154 X

HSG140 *Safe use and handling of flammable liquids* HSE Books 1996 ISBN 0 7176 0967 7

HSG51 *The storage of flammable liquids in containers* HSE Books 1990 ISBN 0 7176 0481 0

PIAC guidance

Fire safety in the printing industry HSE Books 1992 ISBN 0 11 886375 4

CHAPTER 8 MAINTENANCE

INDG21* *Working on fragile roofs* HSE Books 1984

HSG107 *Maintaining portable and transportable electrical equipment* HSE Books 1994 ISBN 0 7176 0715 1 (due to be revised in 1998)

INDG39(rev)* *Permits-to-work and you* HSE Books 1991

HSG54 *The maintenance, examination and testing of local exhaust ventilation* HSE Books 1990 ISBN 0 11 885438 0

Appendix 1

SAFEGUARDING TERMS

· · · · · · · · · · ·

Audible pre-start warning device - a device (normally automatic on depression of a start or slow crawl control on larger machinery) that delivers a clearly audible signal before start up of the machine. See guidance and diagrams under 'Machine controls' in the 'Safety hazards by process section' of Chapter 5

Contra-rotating rollers/cylinders - rollers/cylinders that rotate towards each other

Crawl - slow speed, where machines can run at crawl speeds with guards open they should be capable of running at slow crawl only (see 'Slow crawl'). Where machines run at crawl speeds with guards in position/closed, the crawl speeds can be in excess of those set out for slow crawl as the crawl in this context is not designed to be a safety feature

Electrosensitive safety system - electrosensitive protective equipment, eg photoelectric safety system

Emergency stop device - readily accessible stop controls intended to effect a rapid response to a potentially dangerous situation. Not designed for use as a stop during normal day to day operation. Common types include mushroom-headed buttons, push bars, pull wire and kick plates

Fail to danger - any failure of the machinery, its associated safeguards, controls or power supply that leaves a machine in a dangerous or unsafe condition

Fail to safety/fail-safe - any failure of the machinery, its associated safeguards, controls or power supply that leaves the machine in a safe condition

Fixed guard - guards that require a tool for removal, eg an Allen key or spanner. Wing nuts or similar are not acceptable. Openings in fixed guards are permissible provided safety reach distances are maintained in accordance with BS EN 294 (see 'Important machinery standards' in the References)

Gap covers - usually curved metal sections designed to be fitted in the gaps of plate and blanket cylinders to create a cylinder of smooth circumference

Guard - a physical barrier that prevents or reduces access to a danger point or area

Guard locking - an additional safety feature of certain interlocked guarding for machines with long rundown times which prevents the guards from being opened until dangerous movement within the guarded area has stopped

Hickey picking - removal of hickeys (pieces of fluff or other foreign bodies), usually from the surface of printing cylinders

Hold-to-run controls (dead man's control) - permit movement of a machine only on continued activation of a control. Hold-to-run control devices should be designed to allow movement limited to a maximum of 25 mm or with a maximum operating speed of 1 m/min or where this would reduce the ability of the machine to perform its function and there would be no substantial increase in hazard movement limited to a maximum of 75 mm or with a maximum operating speed of 5 m/min.

Inch - limited movement. Movement should be limited to 25 mm, or 75 mm where this is not possible and does not increase the hazards substantially. Inching is not continuous motion under hold-to-run control

In-running nip - trapping and drawing-in hazard created by rotating rollers or cylinders. Can occur between two contra-rotating rollers (powered or non-powered); one rotating roller and a stationary roller or adjacent fixed part of the machine; rollers rotating in the same direction but with different peripheral speeds or surface properties (friction); guide rollers and driving belts, conveyor belts and possibly the web

Integrity - the ability of devices, systems and procedures to perform their function without failure or defeat

Interlock - a safety device that interconnects a guard with the control system or the power system of the machine

Interlocked guard - a guard that when opened operates an interlock to stop movement of dangerous parts before they can be reached by an operator or other person

Isolate - the removal of all sources of energy in a secure manner, ie by ensuring that inadvertent reconnection is not possible

Lift out/pop out rollers - rollers that are not fixed in position and are light enough to lift out of position if a blockage or entanglement occurs without causing injury

Multi-manned presses - presses designed to be operated by more than one person

Nip bar - fixed section, normally metal, either round or angled, running along the length of rollers or cylinders situated no more than 6 mm from the cylinder or roller surface designed to minimise the risk of entanglement by the nip created by contra-rotating rollers

Safe by position - out of reach. See also safety reach distances in BS EN 294 (see 'Important machinery standards' in the References section)

Safe system of work or safe working practice - a method of working that

eliminates or reduces the risk of injury

Safety device/protective device - a device other than a guard that eliminates or reduces danger

Safety reach distance - safety distance that should prevent dangerous parts from being reached by operators or others

Slow crawl - safety-related restricted operating speed. As a rule, the slow crawl speed should be set at a maximum operating speed of 1 m/min, or 5 m/min where this is not possible because it would reduce the ability of the machine to perform its function and where there would be no substantial increase in hazard

Slow speed - production crawl (with guards in position) - see also 'Crawl'

Trip devices - devices which bring dangerous parts of machinery to rest when activated (eg knocked) by operators or other people

Trip nip bar - similar to a fixed nip bar but when deflected acts to cut the power supply to the motor, causing the press to come to a rapid but controlled stop. The withdrawal path/deflection of the trip bar should be longer than the stopping path of the hazardous movement

Tunnel guard - fixed or interlocked guard that prevents access to dangerous parts using the principles of safety reach distances in construction of the guard, often using a tunnel shape

Two-hand-control - controls designed so that simultaneous operation of the controls (within approximately 0.5 seconds) is required before the machine will operate. Operation of the machine by such controls should usually allow limited movement, eg a single stroke of a guillotine, or movement at slow crawl speeds only. Hazardous movement should stop when either actuator/control is released

Wander lead control/pendant control - portable control panel usually on flexible armoured cable lead allowing operation of the machine from different positions. If the control allows operation of the machine with guards open it should operate as a two-hand-control (see 'Two-hand-control' above)

Web-driven rollers - non-powered rollers that act as if powered due to the driving force of the web

Zoning - each control only allows operation of a limited press or associated area with a guard open when guards elsewhere that are not clearly visible are closed, eg at print units of larger presses

Appendix 2
EXAMPLE RISK ASSESSMENT FORM

■ ■ ■ ■ ■ ■ ■ ■ ■ ■ ■ ■

RISK ASSESSMENT	NO		
Site	Area		
Operations covered by the assessment			
Maximum number of people exposed:			
Frequency and duration of exposure:			
Hazards			
Action already taken to reduce risk	Residual risk		
		Likelihood	Severity
Hazards still outstanding			
Assessment of residual risk: low/medium/high			
Further actions required:		Person responsible	Date completed
Signed: Position:	Date	Review date	
Responsible Director's approval		Date	

This is a suggested risk assessment form. You do not have to use this - it is merely an example of the sort of form you may use

Printed and published by the Health and Safety Executive   C100   3/98

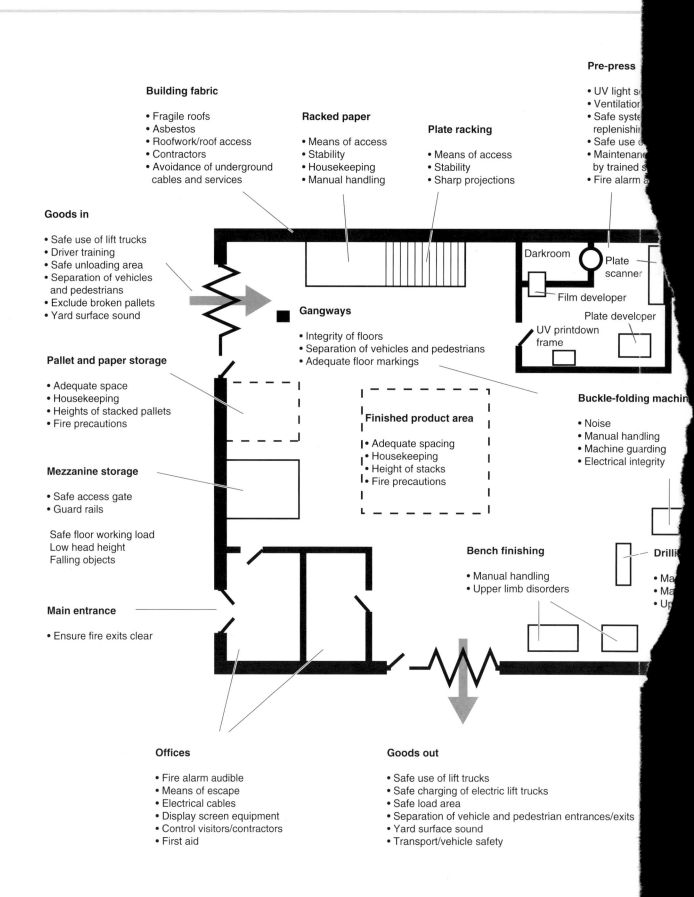

Building fabric

- Fragile roofs
- Asbestos
- Roofwork/roof access
- Contractors
- Avoidance of underground cables and services

Racked paper

- Means of access
- Stability
- Housekeeping
- Manual handling

Plate racking

- Means of access
- Stability
- Sharp projections

Pre-press

- UV light so
- Ventilation
- Safe syste replenishir
- Safe use o
- Maintenan by trained s
- Fire alarm

Goods in

- Safe use of lift trucks
- Driver training
- Safe unloading area
- Separation of vehicles and pedestrians
- Exclude broken pallets
- Yard surface sound

Darkroom

Plate scanner

Film developer

Plate developer

UV printdown frame

Gangways

- Integrity of floors
- Separation of vehicles and pedestrians
- Adequate floor markings

Pallet and paper storage

- Adequate space
- Housekeeping
- Heights of stacked pallets
- Fire precautions

Finished product area

- Adequate spacing
- Housekeeping
- Height of stacks
- Fire precautions

Buckle-folding machin

- Noise
- Manual handling
- Machine guarding
- Electrical integrity

Mezzanine storage

- Safe access gate
- Guard rails

Safe floor working load
Low head height
Falling objects

Bench finishing

- Manual handling
- Upper limb disorders

Drilli

- Ma
- Ma
- Up

Main entrance

- Ensure fire exits clear

Offices

- Fire alarm audible
- Means of escape
- Electrical cables
- Display screen equipment
- Control visitors/contractors
- First aid

Goods out

- Safe use of lift trucks
- Safe charging of electric lift trucks
- Safe load area
- Separation of vehicle and pedestrian entrances/exits
- Yard surface sound
- Transport/vehicle safety

Appendix 3

ASSESSING HAZARDS IN A SMALL PRINT WORKS

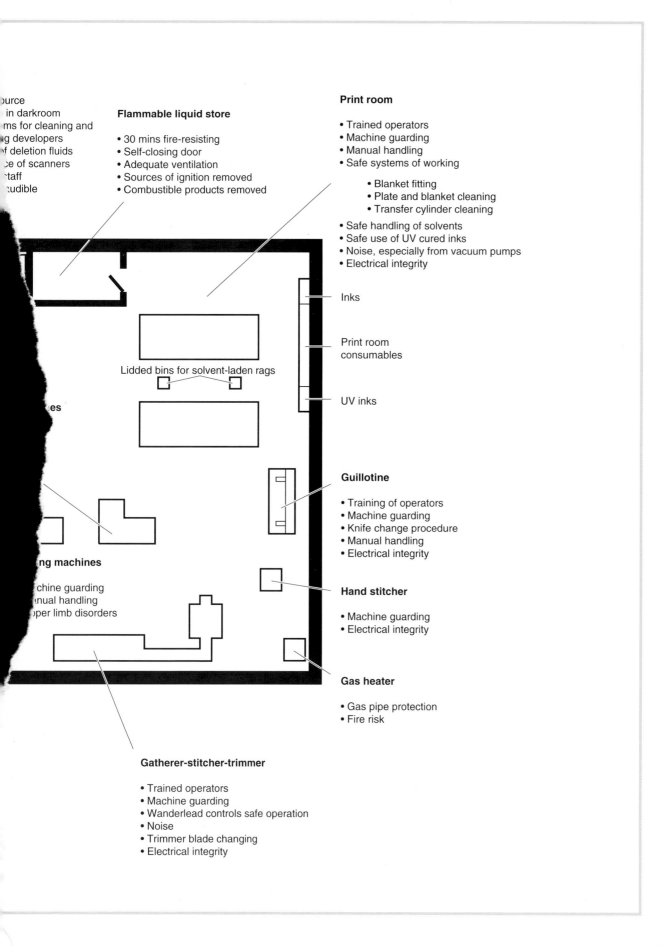

ource
 in darkroom
ms for cleaning and
g developers
f deletion fluids
ce of scanners
taff
udible

Flammable liquid store

• 30 mins fire-resisting
• Self-closing door
• Adequate ventilation
• Sources of ignition removed
• Combustible products removed

Print room

• Trained operators
• Machine guarding
• Manual handling
• Safe systems of working

  • Blanket fitting
  • Plate and blanket cleaning
  • Transfer cylinder cleaning

• Safe handling of solvents
• Safe use of UV cured inks
• Noise, especially from vacuum pumps
• Electrical integrity

Inks

Print room
consumables

UV inks

Lidded bins for solvent-laden rags

es

Guillotine

• Training of operators
• Machine guarding
• Knife change procedure
• Manual handling
• Electrical integrity

ng machines

chine guarding
nual handling
per limb disorders

Hand stitcher

• Machine guarding
• Electrical integrity

Gas heater

• Gas pipe protection
• Fire risk

Gatherer-stitcher-trimmer

• Trained operators
• Machine guarding
• Wanderlead controls safe operation
• Noise
• Trimmer blade changing
• Electrical integrity